The Art of Post-Tonal Analysis

The Art of Post-Tonal Analysis

Thirty-Three Graphic Music Analyses

JOSEPH N. STRAUS

OXFORD

UNIVERSITY PRESS

OXFORD
UNIVERSITY PRESS

Oxford University Press is a department of the University of Oxford. It furthers
the University's objective of excellence in research, scholarship, and education
by publishing worldwide. Oxford is a registered trade mark of Oxford University
Press in the UK and certain other countries.

Published in the United States of America by Oxford University Press
198 Madison Avenue, New York, NY 10016, United States of America.

CIP data is on file at the Library of Congress
ISBN 978–0–19–754398–6 (pbk.)
ISBN 978–0–19–754397–9 (hbk.)

DOI: 10.1093/oso/9780197543979.001.0001

1 3 5 7 9 8 6 4 2

Paperback printed by Marquis, Canada
Hardback printed by Bridgeport National Bindery, Inc., United States of America

Contents

Preface

In this book, I analyze thirty-three musical passages (usually opening passages) or entire short works in a variety of post-tonal styles. For each piece I try to show how it is put together and what sense might be made of it: how the music goes. Along the way, I hope to show the value of post-tonal theory in addressing these questions, and in revealing something of the fascination and beauty of this music.

Repertoire. The works under study are taken from throughout the long twentieth century, from 1909 to the present. Within the atonal wing of modern classical music, the composers discussed here, some canonical and some not, represent a diversity of musical style, chronology, geography, gender, and race/ethnicity.

Graphic analyses. Musical examples, usually incorporating score with analytical annotations, carry the burden of the analytical argument. There is relatively little prose, rarely more than a few sentences at a time. I try to show rather than tell. As the subtitle of this book suggests, I have in mind Heinrich Schenker's *Five Graphic Music Analyses* (Dover, 1969) as a model.

Analytical videos. The website for this book contains video versions of all thirty-three analyses. In these videos, the analytical annotations appear as real-time animations, coordinated with the sounding music. These videos are not a mere supplement to the printed book; rather, the book you hold in your hands should be understood as a static version of the dynamic analytical process that unfolds dramatically in these videos. You can find the videos here: www.oup.com/us/theartofposttonalanalysis.

Pedagogical orientation. In writing these analyses, I imagine I am teaching these pieces to a class of undergraduate or graduate students, seated at the piano, pointing at score, playing and listening as we go. The book and the videos are intended as a record of these (hypothetical) classes. The title of this book pays homage to a book that was produced in just that way: Carl Schachter, *The Art of Tonal Analysis: Twelve Lessons in Schenkerian Theory* (Oxford University Press, 2016).

Audience. This book is aimed at advanced undergraduates, graduate students, and music professionals. I try to explain things as I go, but some basic grasp of post-tonal theory will be useful. To help things along, I have provided a **Post-Tonal Primer** at the back of the book—a quick and dirty introduction to the relevant theoretical concepts.

How to use this book (and the accompanying videos). Readers (and viewers) are encouraged to graze and browse. It is not designed to be read through: there is no narrative arc (the organization is strictly chronological) and no graduation of difficulty. Rather, each analysis is designed to be self-contained. This book is a smorgasbord, an all-you-can-eat buffet, not a formal sit-down meal, served course by course, from soup to nuts.

Bibliography. In lieu of footnotes, the bibliographies at the back of the book acknowledge my intellectual debts and offer recommendations for further reading.

Methodology. I approach these pieces from the various angles and techniques that cumulatively are known as post-tonal theory. Although I deal in passing with character, affect, text setting, rhythm, and form, the primary focus of these analyses is pitch, including intervals, motives, collections, melody, harmony, and voice leading. My approach could be loosely described as transformational. I am interested in seeing how musical ideas (shapes, intervals, motives) grow, change, and effloresce. When musical ideas are obviously dissimilar and possibly in conflict, I am interested in teasing out subtle points of connection between them. Above all, I am interested in creating rich networks of relatedness, allowing our musical minds and musical ears to lead each other along some of the many enjoyable pathways through this challenging and beautiful music.

Acknowledgments. The analytical videos that accompany this book and the musical examples that appear in it were created by Tim Mastic, a graduate student at the CUNY Graduate Center, where I teach. In producing these visual images and multi-sensory animations, Tim not only realized an extraordinarily powerful way of conveying analytical information, but directly shaped the content of the analyses themselves. He has been a brilliant and indispensable collaborator. At a late stage, Austin Lewellen expertly prepared the musical examples for the Post-Tonal Primer. At Oxford University Press, I received enthusiastic support for this enterprise at every stage from a superb editorial team headed originally by Suzanne Ryan and, more recently, by Norman Hirschy. I also benefitted from incisive critical comments from two anonymous reviewers. This is the eleventh book I have written. As with its ten predecessors, I take this opportunity to acknowledge Sally Goldfarb, whose love gives meaning to this work, and to everything I do.

About the Companion Website and Analytical Videos

www.oup.com/us/theartofposttonalanalysis

Oxford has created a website to accompany *The Art of Post-Tonal Analysis: Thirty-Three Graphic Music Analyses.* Here you will find video versions of all thirty-three analyses in which the analytical annotations appear as real-time animations, co-ordinated with the sounding music. We encourage you to consult this resource in conjunction with the chapters.

1

Arnold Schoenberg, *Piano Pieces,* Op. 11, No. 1 (1909)

This passage is arranged as a small ternary form, ABA, with the B material repeated (with variation) three times. The A material involves a simple melody
accompanied by two three-note chords. In the first A section, the melody droops
downward, ending with a descending semitone, F–E (possibly suggesting a traditional musical emblem of lament). The second A section also mostly descends,
and also ends with a semitone (ascending in this case). The B material is a bit more
contrapuntal, with four distinct registral lines that shift in relation to each other.
The cumulative effect is of something restrained and austere, possibly tending toward melancholy.

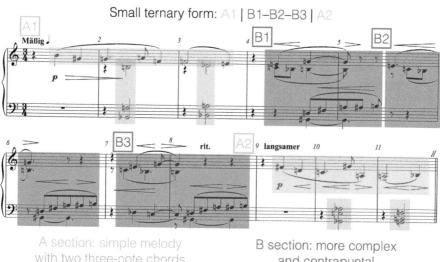

As we look for a point of entry into the piece, we note that the first three melody
notes, B–G♯–G, return as the repeated harmony in the B section, increasingly
fragmented amid its three-fold repetition. The recurrence of B–G♯–G forms a link
between the contrasting A and B sections.

The Art of Post-Tonal Analysis. Joseph N. Straus, Oxford University Press. © Joseph N. Straus 2022.
DOI: 10.1093/oso/9780197543979.003.0001

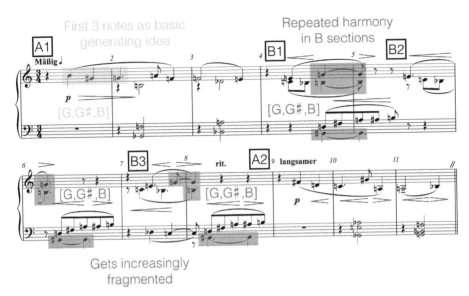

The same three-note idea is repeated (and sometimes varied) in other parts of the passage. Over a larger musical span, the highest notes in each of the three phrases of the passage are the same as the first three pitches of the piece: B–G♯–G, although not in that order.

Each note in that large-scale registral statement is associated with a small scale-statement of the same type of trichord, (014). That is, each of these harmonies is related by transposition or inversion to the opening three-note melodic idea. In that way, we can hear the resonance of the opening three-note melody extending across the passage and downward into the accompanying lines and chords.

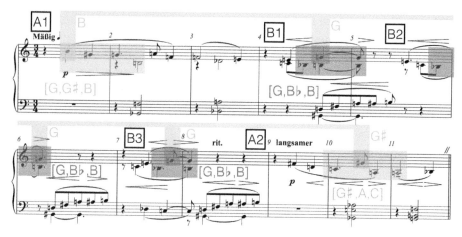

Each high note associated with trichord (014)

Furthermore, the T and I that connect these small-scale statements replicate the T and I that connect the notes within the large-scale registral statement (and within the first three notes of the melody).

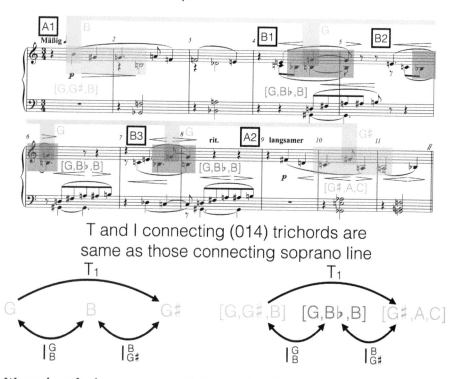

We can hear further resonance with the opening three-note melody if we consider the possibility that it might be varied intervallically without losing its basic identity.

Within the melody of the first A section, the first three notes (B–G♯–G) trace the intervals -3 and -1. The next three notes (A–F–E) expand the first of those intervals by one semitone: now -4 and -1. When the A music returns at the end of the passage, the second interval is expanded by one semitone: now -4 and -2. This systematic process of interval expansion links the first and second A sections. These expanded motivic statements cut across the articulative slurs: the traditional rhetoric of the passage—with a mostly stepwise descending melody grouped as five notes plus two notes—slightly conceals the initial three-note grouping and its emanations.

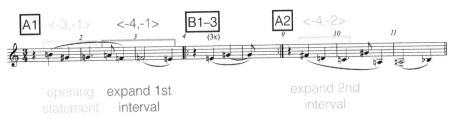

The intervals of the opening motive, 3 and 1, are heard three more times in the melody, only now the intervals move in opposite directions rather than the same direction. The first two of these varied statements (F–E–G and E–G–F♯) connect the B section with the surrounding A sections, linking them in an RI-chain. These motive statements bridge across the silences that separate the A and B sections. The third of these varied statements leads to the final note of the melody (momentarily ignoring the high-register G♯).

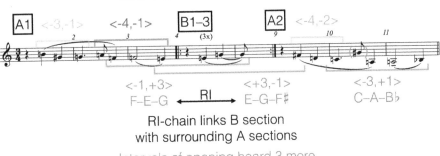

A slightly more distant intervallic echo is heard in the relationship between the first three notes and the three notes in measure 10: C–G♯–A. As pitch-class sets, they are related by transposition by semitone—one of the intervals of the generating three-note motive.

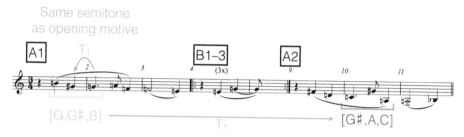

Pitch class sets of opening and m. 10
related by semitone transposition

The same intervallic relationship, T_1, is felt between the large-scale motivic statement in the melody and a similar large-scale statement in the bass. The two large-scale statements are related at T_1, which is also part of the opening three-note melody itself, as G-to-G♯.

The basic three-note melodic idea helps to shape the chords as well as the melodic lines. In the first A section, the three-note melody returns, transposed and rearranged, as the second chord. In the second A section, the expanded three-note melody similarly returns, transposed and rearranged, as the second chord.

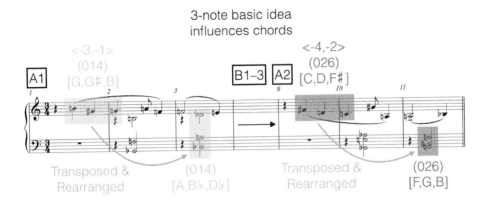

The four-chord progression as a whole takes us away from and very nearly back to our starting point. The chords may be heard to move by near-transposition, where two out of the three notes are transposed in the usual way, while the third note deviates. The deviations are small, and the first and the last chords are almost identical (the one deviating note is off by only a semitone, that familiar motivic interval). In the melody and in the chords, the first three notes, B–G#–G, and their intervals thus resonate throughout the passage.

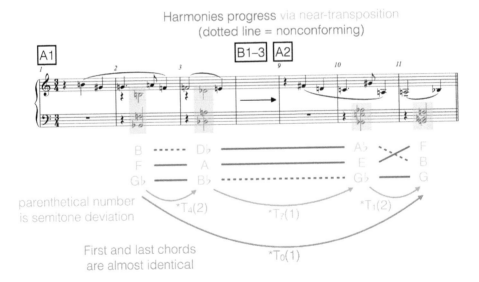

2

Anton Webern, *Movements for String Quartet,* Op. 5, No. 2 (1909)

Only three members of the string quartet are playing in this passage: a poignant, yearning melody in the viola is accompanied by chords in the second violin and cello. The first three melody notes, G–B–C♯, return as the chord at the end of the passage. That chord has a cadential feel, as though the melody and chords were directed toward the return of the first three notes. We will try to figure out why.

The second of the three accompanying chords is related to the third chord by transposition at T_4. That harmonic gesture replicates the T_4 relationship between the first two notes of the melody, G–B. That particular pair of T_4-related notes, G–B, is also found in the bass register of the harmonic progression.

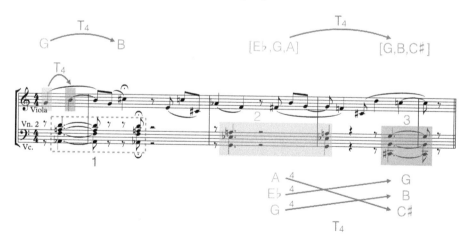

The Art of Post-Tonal Analysis. Joseph N. Straus, Oxford University Press. © Joseph N. Straus 2022.
DOI: 10.1093/oso/9780197543979.003.0002

The melody contains two additional forms of the same set class, (026), and these are related by inversion around the F–G they share.

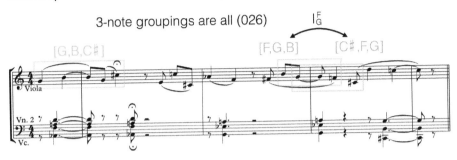

We have now identified five forms of (026) in this passage. Taking the three different transpositionally related forms of (026) in the passage, we note that they are connected by the same intervals of transposition (2, 4, and 6) as the intervals formed among the notes of the motive itself.

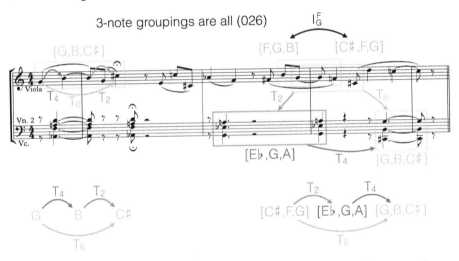

In the whole passage, we can identify three melodic and three harmonic forms of (026).

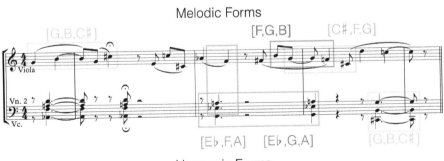

In both melody and harmony, it is possible to link the forms of (026) into an RI-chain that binds them and directs the motion toward the concluding [G, B, C♯]. That final chord feels cadential because it is both a return to the opening three notes and the culminating arrival of two RI-chains of (026).

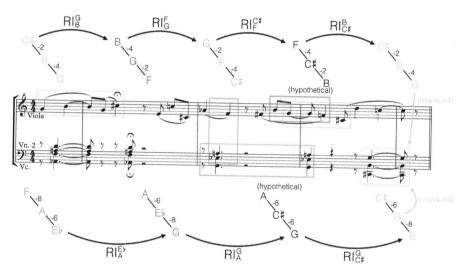

The final chord can also be understood as the conclusion of a three-chord progression in the accompaniment. The progression involves a fuzzy-T_1 and a crisp-T_4 combining to create a fuzzy-T_5 that spans the passage.

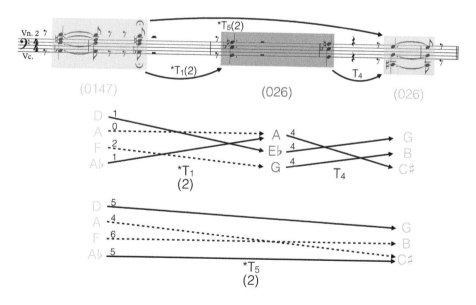

The same constellation of intervals (1, 4, and 5) resonates in the melody also, both
in its smaller intervallic cells and the final notes of each of its three phrases. Just as
the final chord is the culmination of a harmonic process, the final melody note is the
culmination of a melodic process.

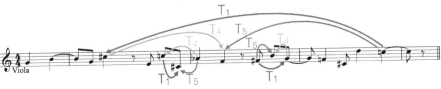

3

Alban Berg, "Schlafend trägt man mich," from *Four Songs*, Op. 2, No. 2 (1910)

The harmonies in this passage can be thought of as a progression of six chords leading to a repeat of the first chord.

(Text Translation: Sleeping I am carried back to my homeland)

The six chords represent the six distinct forms of (0268). The set is highly symmetrical (that's why the set class has so few members), and adjacent chords can be related by transposition in two different ways: T_{11} or T_5.

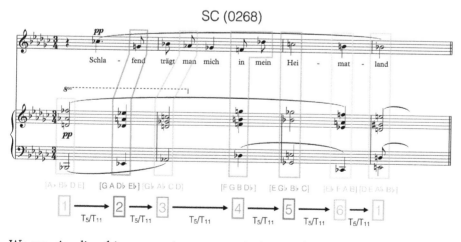

We can visualize this progression on a musical space for (0268). Of the six sets in (0268), three belong to WT_0 (the whole-tone scale that contains C) and three belong

The Art of Post-Tonal Analysis. Joseph N. Straus, Oxford University Press. © Joseph N. Straus 2022.
DOI: 10.1093/oso/9780197543979.003.0003

to WT$_1$ (the whole-tone scale that contains C#). Each set is connected by two possible transpositions to the adjacent sets in this space.

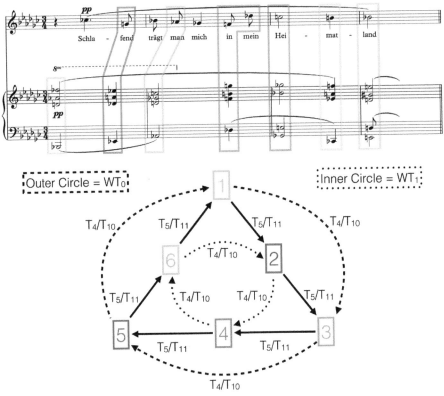

The motion of the registral lines frequently reflects either the T$_5$ or T$_{11}$ relationships. The bass moves exclusively by T$_5$ (up by perfect fourth or down by perfect fifth); the upper voices move by T$_{11}$ (usually down by semitone, with an occasional leap up by major seventh).

Registral lines move by T$_5$ or T$_{11}$

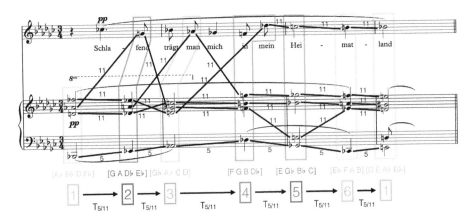

Indeed, the voices mostly conform to a systematic voice-leading scheme, with the bass moving at T_5 and the upper four voices moving at T_{11}. In every chord, one of the upper four notes doubles the bass note. The only exception is the first chord, where the melodic C♭ displaces the B♭ that would fit into the scheme. The idea that C♭ usurps the place that in a sense should be occupied by B♭ is one to which we will return.

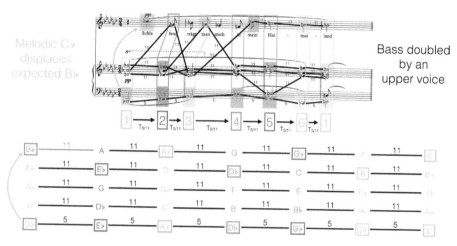

Voice-Leading Matrix of T_5 and T_{11}

The progression carries us away from home, through a journey that takes in all possible forms of the chord, and finally carries us back home—a subtle and effective reflection of the text.

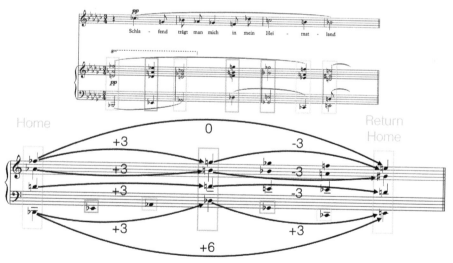

(Text Translation: Sleeping I am carried back to my homeland)

The melody consists largely of an RI-chain involving (015). Having enchained its way from the opening C♭ to C♮, the melody then descends to its close on B♭.

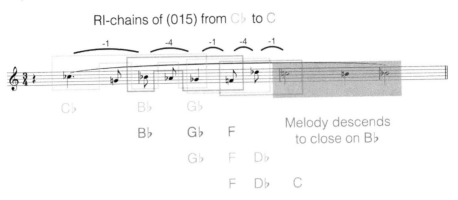

The initial C♭ is felt as an appoggiatura (we previously noted the sense in which it displaces an expected B♭). It does not belong to the sounding form of (0268), unlike most of the melody notes, and it seems to resolve to B♭. The same motion is heard at the end of the line and over the course of the whole melody. In this hearing, B♭ as a melody tone, like the first chord as a harmony, represents the homeland toward which the music moves.

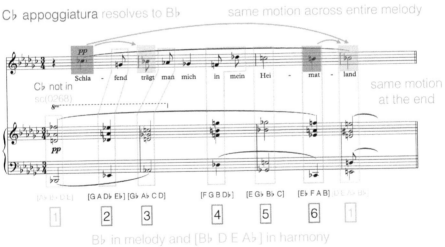

4

Igor Stravinsky, *The Rite of Spring,* Introduction to Part I (1913)

The Rite of Spring begins with a haunting, diatonic melody high in the bassoon, harmonized in an unusual, dissonant fashion by other wind and brass instruments.

The bassoon melody is based closely on a Russian folk melody. On its own terms, the melody would probably be understood in the key of A minor, or perhaps the Aeolian mode (without a raised leading tone), organized with reference to a descending minor third, C–B–A.

The Art of Post-Tonal Analysis. Joseph N. Straus, Oxford University Press. © Joseph N. Straus 2022.
DOI: 10.1093/oso/9780197543979.003.0004

But Stravinsky's harmonization conflicts strongly with the A minor implications of the melody. He harmonizes the melody first with C♯ alone and then with the perfect fourth G♯–C♯.

In relation to that perfect fourth, the melody is arranged symmetrically: the inversion that maps G♯ onto C♯ also maps D onto G and C onto A.

Understood in that way, we can hear the motion from C to A not as a third-progression in A minor but in response to the pressure exerted by G♯–C♯: the C seeks and finds its symmetrical partner, thus restoring inversional balance and closing the gesture.

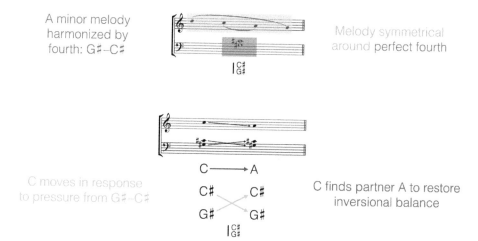

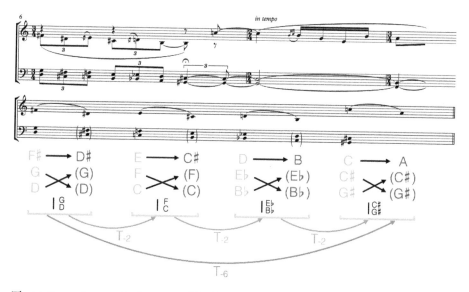

The same voice-leading gesture—a descending minor third in the upper voice heard with reference to a framing perfect fourth—is heard three times in measures 6–7. It's a sequential motion: each pair of inversionally related chords is transposed down two semitones, traversing a total span of a tritone, and leading to a return of the opening melody.

That tritone descent is the second half of an octave descent that begins in measure 4. Within these larger transpositional gestures, the local voice leading is often via inversion, and often involves a descending minor third in the upper voice. At the highest level, we can hear the entire passage as an upper-voice motion from C to A, supported by a sustained perfect fourth, G♯-C♯, and motivated by $I_{G\sharp}^{C\sharp}$.

At the end of the passage (measures 10–12), the accompanying perfect fourth, G♯-C♯, is sustained in the bass. The folk tune is gone now, replaced by a more spacious new melody. But the new melody still descends by minor third (F♯–D♯) and that melodic descent is still inversionally symmetrical with respect to $I_{G\sharp}^{C\sharp}$.

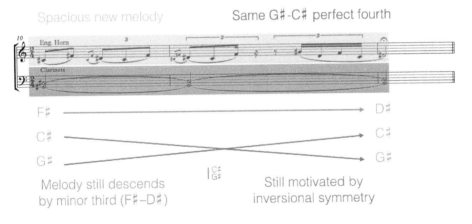

Taking the two parts of the passage together, we find a single unifying gesture in the melody, traversing a complete cycle of minor thirds: C–A–F♯–D♯.

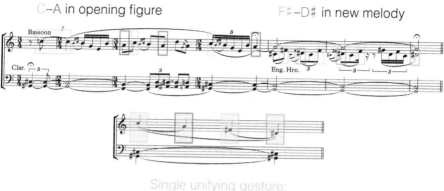

One can imagine the passage as working out a clash between two structural perfect fifths: C♯-G♯ and D-A. C♯-G♯ is represented by the sustained perfect fourth in the accompaniment and by the new melody that arrives in measure 10. D-A is represented by the melodic tetrachord D-C-B-A, within which the folk melody unfolds. In traditional, tonal music, the melody and harmony coincide and support each other. In this passage, however, the melody and the harmony, each centered on its own referential perfect fifth, are in tension with each other. The fact that the structural fifths are a dissonant semitone apart intensifies the clash between them.

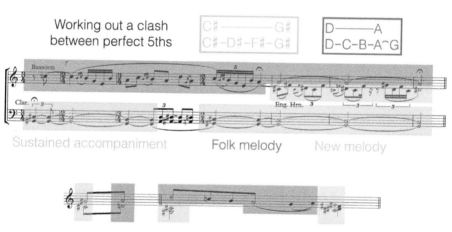

Semitone between fifths enhances clash

5

Igor Stravinsky, *Three Pieces* for string quartet, No. 2 (1914)

This work is highly sectionalized, often with silences separating the sections, and, within each section, highly repetitive.

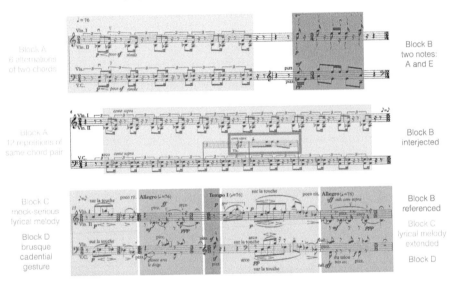

Block A sounds trudging, limping, heavily laden. It consists of two chords of the same type: (0156). Each chord can be thought of as two perfect fifths a semitone apart. The first chord pairs A-E with the perfect fifth a semitone higher (B♭-F); the second chord pairs A-E with the perfect fifth a semitone lower (A♭-E♭). The two chords together are symmetrical around the A-E they share.

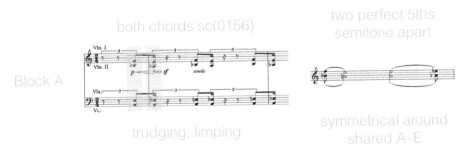

The Art of Post-Tonal Analysis. Joseph N. Straus, Oxford University Press. © Joseph N. Straus 2022.
DOI: 10.1093/oso/9780197543979.003.0005

It is possible to think of the two chords as related by transposition, with the second chord a semitone lower than the first. From that point of view, the descending semitone in the soprano and tenor is a direct manifestation of the T_{11} that connects the chords.

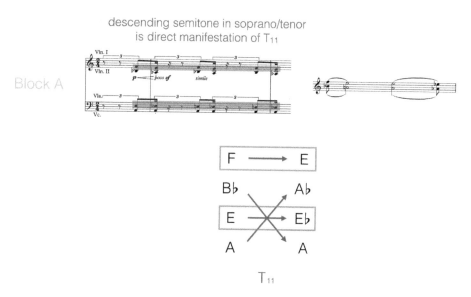

But it may be more productive to think of them as related by inversion at I_E^A, that is, the inversion that exchanges A and E. In this sense, these two chords together establish A-E as a stable, structural perfect fifth, one which is literally central in the passage: everything balances around it.

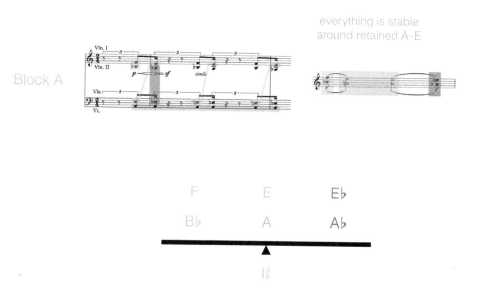

The B music consists of just two notes, A and E. As we just saw, these are the common tones between the two chords in the A-music, the notes around which those chords balance. Now, in the B music, those two central tones stand alone. There's at least a hint here that the A is a sort of tonic, possibly of A minor. This is a possibility I'll explore more a bit later.

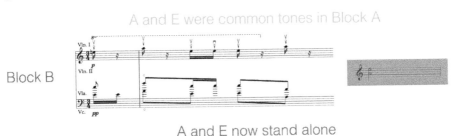

The C music is a lyrical melody played in octaves. It contrasts sharply in mood with the earlier music, especially with the alternating chords in the A music. The chords trudge along, and never get anywhere, as if immobilized by having to carry some sort of heavy burden. This melody seems to sing, and covers a fairly wide expanse. It strikes me as deliberately over-sentimental, as if someone is only pretending to weep. In any case, it begins and ends as abruptly as the trudging chords did. And it has another affinity with the trudging chords, namely an orientation toward the perfect fifth, A-E, and toward a sense of inversional balance around those notes.

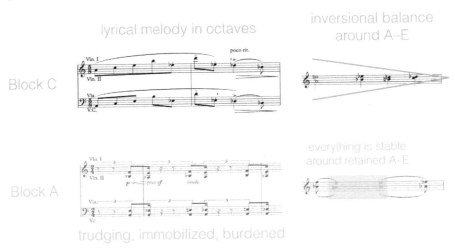

Each note of the melody is positioned near its inversional partner—the notes appear to seek, and eventually find, their inversional partners with respect to A and E. The melody begins by arpeggiating an A-minor triad, another hint of that tonality, and ends on B♭—that will become important in just a moment. For now, however, the music maintains a precarious balance around A-E.

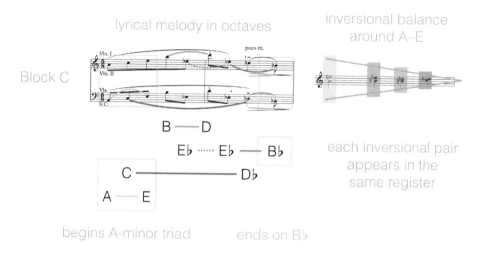

That balance is abruptly toppled by the D music, which is centered on the structural fifth B♭-F, amid repeated motions from F in the bass to B♭ in the upper voice that evoke a V–I cadential motion. The B♭ is always dissonated by the C♭ that invariably sounds with it.

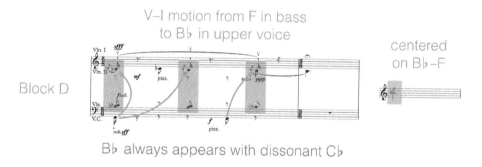

In the opening chord of the piece, the fifth A-E was conjoined with B♭-F. But the A-E was clearly primary, and the B♭-F was secondary, poised above it just as the A♭-E♭ of the second chord was poised below it. Then in music that followed, A-E was maintained as both a centric focus and as an inversional fulcrum around with other elements balanced. In the cadential D music, however, the A-E fifth is abruptly banished, and the B♭-F is violently asserted as the new focal point.

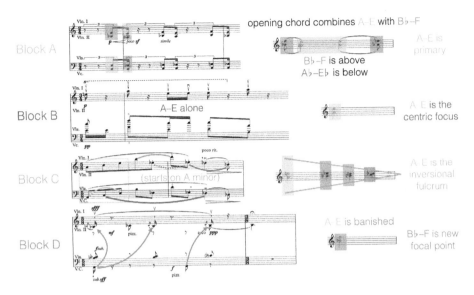

This may seem a strange way to end a passage. Instead of returning to the tonality of the beginning, as traditional tonal pieces do, this passage ends with an abrupt departure. Instead of a reassuring return we get a sharp kick in the rear end, and the door slams behind us.

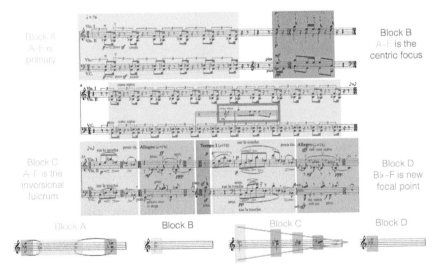

I have suggested that there are hints in this piece of traditional tonality. We might take those hints and try to reconstruct a hypothetical, normalized tonal progression that might be heard to underlie Stravinsky's passage. Beneath the two-chord progression of Stravinsky's A fragment, I imagine a simple 5–6 or $\frac{5}{3}$ to $\frac{6}{4}$ motion above a stationary A. I'm hearing Stravinsky's melodic F–E as the familiar *seufzer* or sighing figure that resolves scale-degree $\hat{6}$ to $\hat{5}$ in minor. I imagine Stravinsky's B fragment, with its leaps from E to A and back, as suggesting a simple V–I progression in A minor, and I imagine Stravinsky's lyrical melody in the C fragment as being harmonized the same way. A simple cadence in A minor becomes the abrupt, B♭-oriented termination of Block D. In relation to the hypothetical prototype, Stravinsky's actual composition is a radical transformation. In its antagonistic relationship to the formal and harmonic norms of traditional tonality, static textural blocks and formal fragmentation replace goal-oriented coherent tonal progressions.

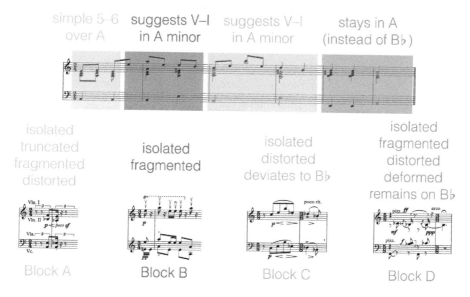

6

Arnold Schoenberg, *Five Piano Pieces,*
Op. 23, No. 3 (1923)

This passage has something of the feel of a Baroque fugue—emotionally restrained and contrapuntally dense. The five-note subject of this apparent fugue is followed immediately by a sort of "fugal answer" at the perfect fifth. The answer enters a beat too soon, before the subject has quite finished. At the end of the passage, the series is heard in inversion, at a level that shares four tones in common with the original series.

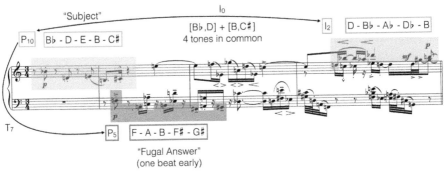

The three forms of the series identified so far are connected by the same T and I that can be found within the series itself—that's what creates the network of common tones that binds the series forms.

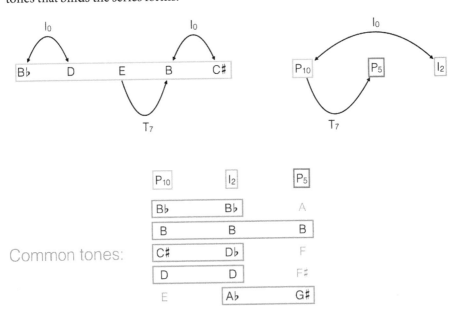

Common tones:	P_{10}	I_2	P_5
	Bb	Bb	A
	B	B	B
	C#	Db	F
	D	D	F#
	E	Ab	G#

The Art of Post-Tonal Analysis. Joseph N. Straus, Oxford University Press. © Joseph N. Straus 2022.
DOI: 10.1093/oso/9780197543979.003.0006

There are two more statements of the series in the passage, both involving discrepancies in the serial ordering. In RI$_5$, which overlaps extensively with P$_{10}$, the final note, F, comes in too soon, as noted earlier. In I$_6$, the last two notes of the series are heard before the first three.

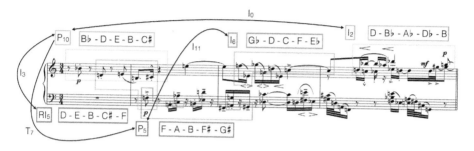

The entire network of five series forms is bound together by the same T and I that bind the notes of the series itself.

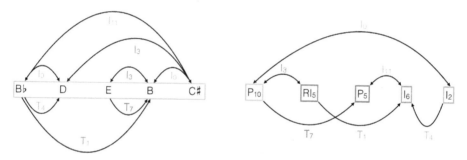

Many additional statements of the series can be found in this passage, but with the ordering so obscured that it is best to think of them as unordered collections. Statements of this collection type, (01346), account for virtually every note in the passage.

Statements of sc(01346)

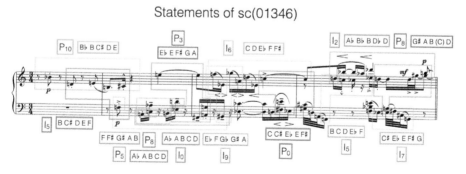

It is possible to bind some of these pentachords into a single network, based on a small number of contextual inversions. J, K, and L are from Lewin (2008). J′, the obverse of J, is my contribution.

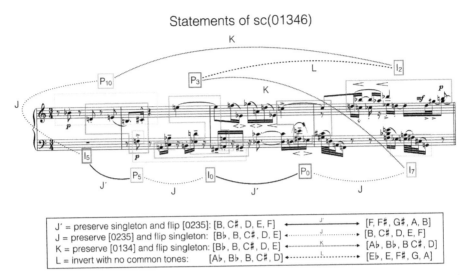

It can be helpful to visualize the progression of these pentachords on a musical space in which the nodes are the members of this pentachord class (written with pitch-class integers in a compressed format) and the lines are the contextual inversions that connect them. From this vantage point, the passage can be thought of as projecting two progressions of pentachords, one mostly higher and the other mostly lower. The lower strand starts on P_{10} then zigzags down and to the right through a chain of J and J′, culminating at I_7. The upper strand also starts on P_{10}, but zigzags up and to the left through a chain of K and L, culminating at the same I_7 (the appearance of I_7 at two different locations in the space is an illusion—in reality the space is a torus, and the two instances of I_7 occur at a single place). One source opening out to two paths then converging onto a single goal. With the profusion of pentachords in the passage, this is far from the only musically meaningful path!

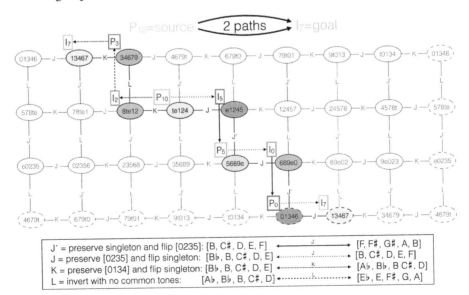

7

Béla Bartók, String Quartet No. 3, *Prima parte* (1927)

This passage consists of a hushed, sustained chord in the lower parts (marked pianissimo and played with mutes) and a whispered, lyrical melody. The melody has a somewhat traditional arch shape: it begins in a halting manner, in a middle register, accelerates toward a high point, and then subsides. The sustained chord in the lower three instruments consists of four notes: C♯-D-D♯-E; the melody in the first violin contains the remaining eight notes. The passage as a whole thus contains all twelve notes, completing the chromatic aggregate.

Despite their pitch complementarity and obvious textural contrast, the melody and the chord have deep affinities. To appreciate them, we begin by looking closely at the melody, taking its first three notes as a basic cell. It is followed immediately by its inversion. The second cell ignites an RI-chain with three links. The third link in the chain is related to the original three notes by inversion around their shared first note, A♮. The first seven notes of the melody—the whole first phrase—thus embed four overlapped motivic cells, related intervallically to the first three notes.

The Art of Post-Tonal Analysis. Joseph N. Straus, Oxford University Press. © Joseph N. Straus 2022.
DOI: 10.1093/oso/9780197543979.003.0007

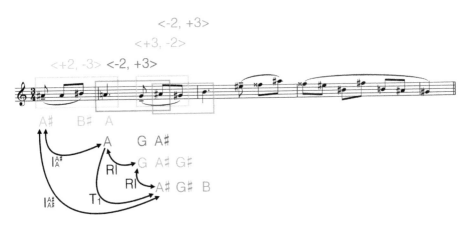

The same motive is composed-out over the entire span of the melody. The three notes of longest duration, A-B-G♯, have the same intervallic shape as the first three notes of the melody, A♯-B♯-A. Each note in this large-scale statement is the third note in a small-scale statement of the motive.

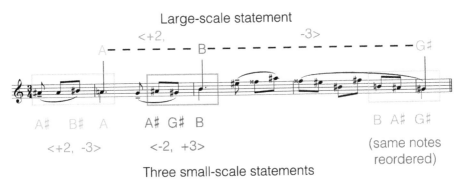

Three small-scale statements

Until now, we have been concerned with intervals 2 and 3 moving in opposite directions. At the top of the melody, however, we hear two retrograde-related statements of a different motive, still using intervals 2 and 3, but in the same direction. We already had a premonition of this motivic variant at the beginning of the melody, in the interstices between two I-related forms of our original three-note motive.

We can represent these first five melody notes as a cycle of pitch classes, starting and ending on A♯, and moving by 2s and 3s. The cycle embeds four trichords: the statements of the original motive, with 2 and 3 moving in opposite directions, represent (013); the statement of the motivic variant, with 2 and 3 moving the same direction, represent (025).

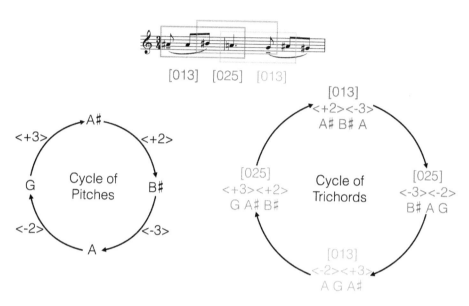

And what of the four-note chord that accompanies this melody? Its notes enter in a particular order: C♯–D–E–D♯. The first three notes, C♯-D-E, consist of a 2 and a 1 moving the same direction, and comprise the set class of our melodic cell: (013). The last three notes, overlapping with these, D-E-D♯, consist of a 2 and a 1 moving in opposite directions, and form a chromatic trichord, (012).

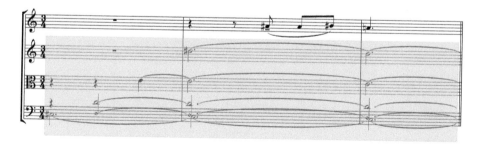

Like the two melodic motives, these overlapping harmonic trichords can be represented as a cycle of pitch classes, combining intervals 1 and 2, or a cycle of sets, with (013) alternating with (012). As we saw, the melody involves intervals 2 and 3 either turning inward, to produce (013) or outward, to produce (025). The chord involves intervals 2 and 1 either turning outward to produce (013), the set class of the melody, or inward to produce (012).

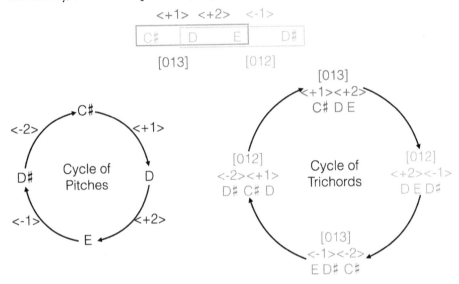

The melody and the chord are related in yet another way, through their shared focus on inversional symmetry on I_5. The chord itself is symmetrical on this axis. In the melody, notes generally occur in close proximity to their inversional partners. More broadly, we might say that the inversional symmetry of the chord exerts pressure on each tone to find its inversional partner, and that this is what impels the A of measure 3, weakly partnered by G♯ in the same measure, to move to the final G♯.

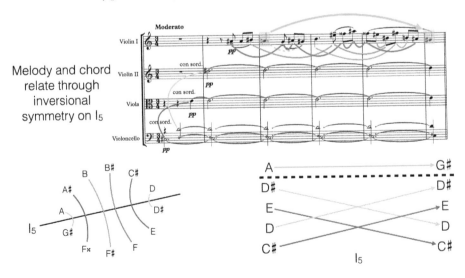

8

Aaron Copland, *Piano Variations, Theme* (1930)

This is the theme for an extended set of variations. But within the theme itself, there is already a great deal of variation with respect to a four-note motto: E–C–D♯–C♯. The two halves of the theme begin with the motto, with the second statement echoed in a canon at the lower octave. The first half is loud and violent, with wide leaps, and punctuated by dissonant *sforzando* chords; the second half is tranquil, with a quieter mood and a more smoothly flowing melodic line.

Leaving out the sharp punctuations and the canonic imitations, we can parse the entire melodic line into a series of six short utterances starting always on E, with the second half an almost exact repeat of the first half. In general, the second half smooths out the contour of the line, maintaining the note succession, but with mostly conjunct motion.

The Art of Post-Tonal Analysis. Joseph N. Straus, Oxford University Press. © Joseph N. Straus 2022.
DOI: 10.1093/oso/9780197543979.003.0008

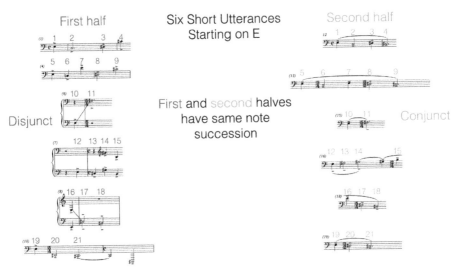

That twenty-one-note melody is in a rough ABA form. In the first A section, we hear two statements of the motive (the second of which has a repeated note). In the B section we hear two contrasting ideas, both of which refer to the notes and intervals of the motive. The concluding A section consists of two truncated statements of the motive.

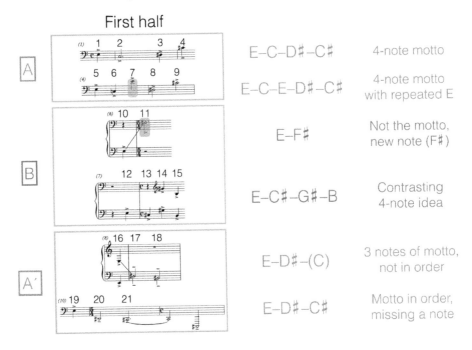

The motto harmony can be thought of in terms of transpositional combination, as 3*1 (i.e., two 3s related by semitone). As the B section begins, the addition of F♯ creates a new tetrachord that can be thought of as 3*2: C♯-E combined with D♯-F♯. As the B section continues, C♯-E is combined with G♯-B as 3*5. There is thus a steady process of intervallic expansion, from the densely chromatic to the intervallically spacious.

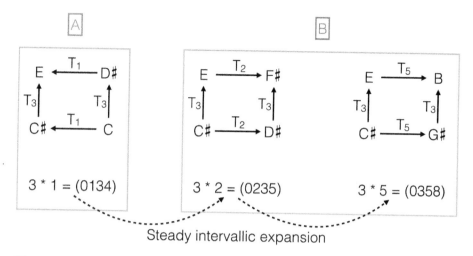

Steady intervallic expansion

The outer sections suggest OCT_{01}; the contrasting middle section contains the five notes of $PENT_E$. Despite the collectional contrast, the A and B sections also share elements in common, most conspicuously the dyad E-F♯, which belongs to both collections and functions as a pivot between them.

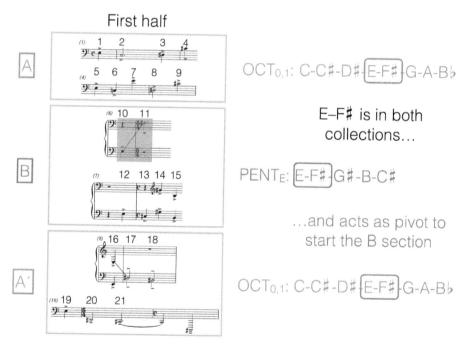

The four-note motto is balanced symmetrically around D.

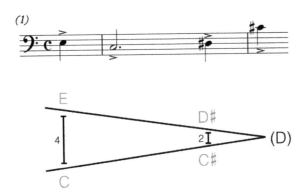

4-note motto symmetrical around implied D

In the first half of the melody, the short melodic fragments are usually punctuated with short, sharp attacks of a single note, a dyad, or a four-note chord. Just as the motto is balanced around D, the two punctuating four-note chords are also related by inversion around D.

Short, sharp attacks punctuate the melodic fragments

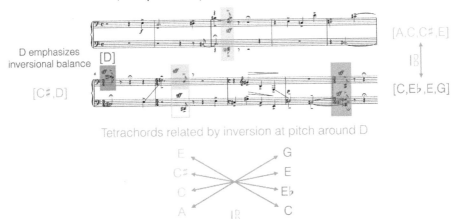

Tetrachords related by inversion at pitch around D

The two punctuating tetrachords, [A, C, C♯, E] and [C, E♭, E, G], can both be thought of as embedding a pair of P-related triads.

Each tetrachord is a pair of P-related triads

More generally, triads play an important role as underlying harmonies in this music, and they are often related by the familiar triadic transformations, including P, L, R, SLIDE, and HEXPOLE. In some cases, the triads are incomplete, but can be easily inferred.

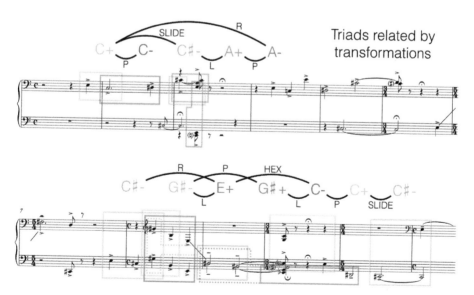

These triads can be traced on a transformational space within which we can hear the progression as a journey away and back. After beginning around C major, C minor, and C♯ minor, the middle section of the melody brings in A♭ major and G♯ minor, and we reach the farthest distance from our starting point (although, in truth, we haven't gone very far at all). The second punctuating chord returns us to the harmonies of the motto, and eventually to C♯ minor, which acts as a sort of global tonic for the piece. The ambiguous, clouded C♯ minor tonality of the passage is implicit in the motto itself, with its unmistakable reference to four notes of C♯ harmonic minor: B♯ (♯7̂), C♯ (1̂), D♯ (2̂), E (3̂). But the C♯ minor triad is adumbrated not via conventional tonal relationship but through a network of triadic transformations, amid a stream of somewhat independent intervallic and motivic development.

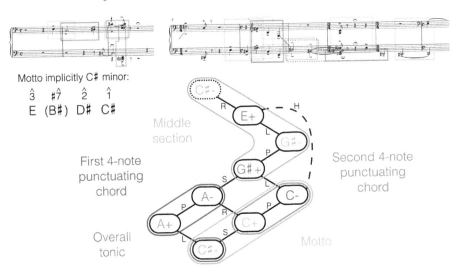

9

Ruth Crawford Seeger, *Diaphonic Suite No. 1*, first movement (1930)

This is the first half of a short movement for solo flute or oboe. It is written in what the composer calls "verse form"—a series of melodic lines, like the lines of a poem, that create a musical rhyme scheme by ending in a similar way. Here, we have two pairs of lines, each marked by a double bar line, in the form ABAB. Rhythmically, lines 1 and 3 are similar, while lines 2 and 4 are identical. The cadential conclusion to all four lines is a leap of 11 semitones—that's the musical rhyme.

"Verse Form" creates musical rhyme with similar endings

Lines 1 and 3 are rhythmically similar

Lines 2 and 4 are rhythmically identical

Rhyme scheme

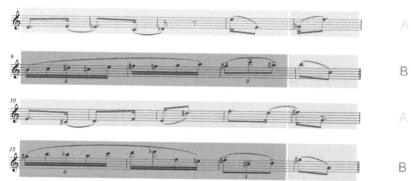

Musical rhyme: leap of 11 semitones

The Art of Post-Tonal Analysis. Joseph N. Straus, Oxford University Press. © Joseph N. Straus 2022.
DOI: 10.1093/oso/9780197543979.003.0009

Let's take the first three notes, D–E–E♭, as a basic motive, describing intervals <+2, –1>. It occupies a small chromatic cluster of semitones, D-E♭-E. It opens a space, then fills it in. It converges on its central tone, E♭, on which it is inversionally symmetrical. As we will see, all of these qualities resonate throughout the melody in various ways.

The basic motive

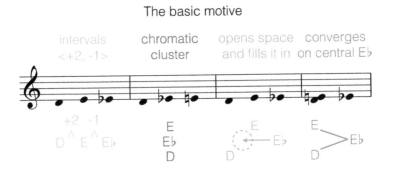

The motive, taken as a series of three notes, can appear in four different orderings (we'll call them P, I, R, and RI).

Motive in four orderings

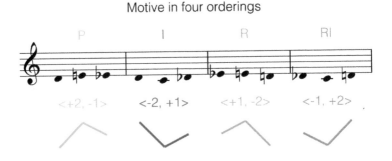

Three of the four orderings can be heard within the first five notes of the melody: the first three notes describe P; the notes on the downbeats of the three measures form R, and the lowest three notes outline I.

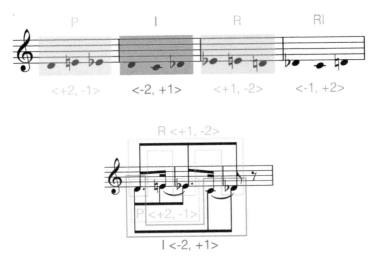

There are many other statements of the motive in the melody, sometimes isolated and sometimes overlapping, sometimes involving three contiguous notes and sometimes slightly extended. Because the motive involves small intervals (1 and 2) moving in opposite directions, it usually conveys the sense of creeping around within a small space, with every move in one direction immediately followed by a slightly smaller or larger move in the other direction.

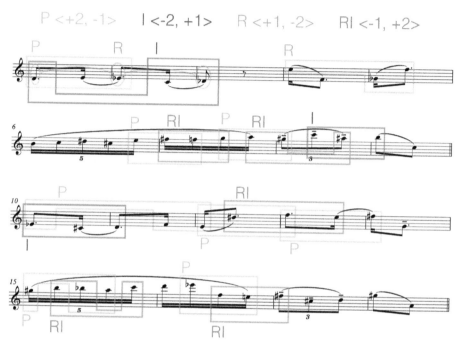

Sometimes we get a sense of the melody creeping slowly in some direction, usually upward. This occurs particularly when this motive, or closely related motives, are bound together into RI-chains. The final chain connects the end of this section of the piece with the beginning of the next one.

RI-chains link upward motion

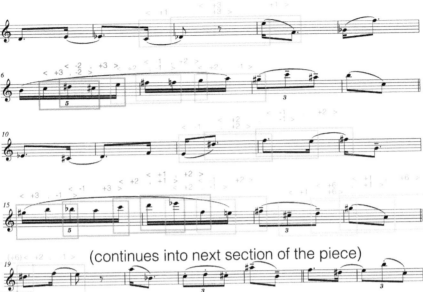

(continues into next section of the piece)

If we think of the motive as an unordered collection rather than an ordered series, we find that the collections are connected via transposition by the same intervals, 1 and 2, that comprise the motive itself. Transposing a set by an interval it contains produces common tones, and these add to the sense of a melody that moves slowly and haltingly through space, amid constant references back to where it has just been.

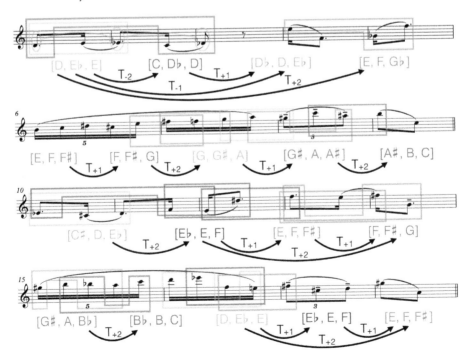

The same is true of the recurring leaps of 11 semitones. They can be thought of as motivic (an expanded representation of interval 1) and they are connected motivically (via intervals 1 and 2).

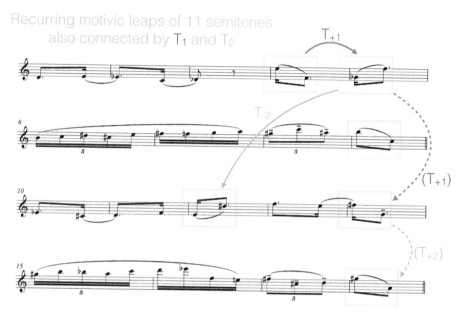

These big leaps punctuate a melody that otherwise does either of two things: remains roughly in place, doubling back on itself; moves decidedly upward, opening up new registral space. In all of this melodic movement, there is an interest in filling musical space: melodic gaps are soon or eventually filled, until virtually every pitch from the lowest to the highest has been heard. The passage as a whole thus does on a large scale what the main motive does in only three notes: open a space and fill it in.

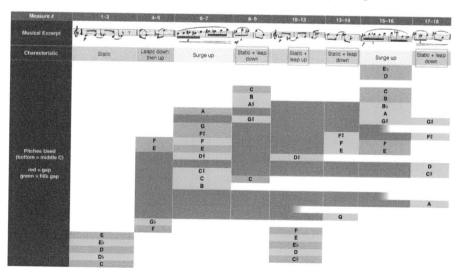

10

Ruth Crawford Seeger, String Quartet, first movement (1931)

This movement juxtaposes contrasting melodies in a texture the composer called "heterophony" (i.e., a particularly intense sort of polyphony, in which the lines are highly differentiated, both in their internal organization and their apparently minimal level of cooperative mutual support). Following her own labeling system, "I" designates the melody in the first violin, "Ia" designates a variant of it in the second violin, and "II" designates a contrasting melody that starts in the cello, then moves to the viola and back to the cello.

I: melody in first violin

II: contrasting melody shared by cello and viola

Ia: variant of melody in second violin

Let's begin by comparing Melodies I and Ia. The contrast between them is striking: I is marked *mezzo piano, cantando*—a flowing, lyrical melody; Ia is marked *forte, marcato bruscamente*—composed of short, heavily accented notes. Both melodies feature wide leaps, and both begin with a descending major seventh, but what else do they have in common? Before we consider their intervals, let's consider their overall shape: their contours and their balance of ascending and descending motion. Both melodies begin with the contour <-, +, +>, that is, a descending motion followed by two ascending motions. The remaining four-note shapes in both melodies either replicate that one or invert it into <+, -, ->, replacing each descending motion by an ascending one, and vice versa.

The Art of Post-Tonal Analysis. Joseph N. Straus, Oxford University Press. © Joseph N. Straus 2022.
DOI: 10.1093/oso/9780197543979.003.0010

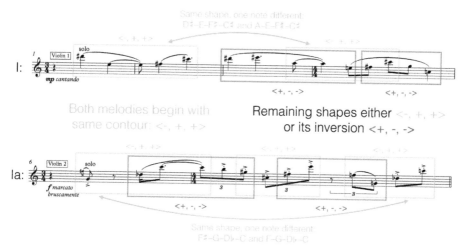

We can refine our sense of shared contour between these melodies by considering their contour segments (CSEGs), a way of naming a contour by assigning 0 to the lowest note, 1 to the second-lowest note, and so on. The two melodies share CSEGs and their variants (inversion, retrograde, and retrograde-inversion). For example, <2310> and its variant forms occur fully seven times across the two melodies. Despite their differences in character, then, these two melodies express similar and related contours.

The two melodies are intervallically distinct: I has mostly 5s and 2s; Ia has mostly 1s and 6s.

Melody I: mostly intervals of 2 and 5

Melody Ia: mostly intervals of 1

But they do share a group of three notes in reverse order: E–F♯–C♯ in I and C♯–F♯–E in Ia. In addition, the first four notes of Ia are heard, in slightly scrambled order, as the last four notes of I and the last three notes of the two melodies are the same, again in scrambled order.

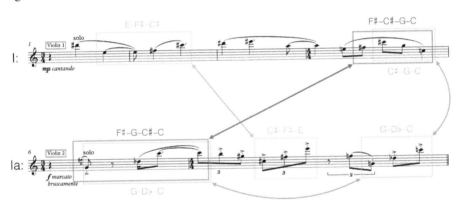

They also share a sense of inversion around D♯/E-A/B♭: in both melodies, notes are often heard in close proximity to their partners on this axis. Some of the inversional pairs are shared between the two melodies: C♯-F♯ and C-G occur in both. Other pairings are distinct: D♯-E occurs twice in I but not in Ia; G♯-B occurs in Ia but not in I.

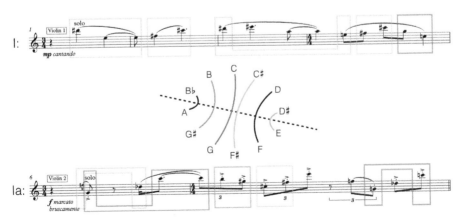

They are both also partitioned registrally into complementary whole-tone collections. In Melody I, the notes from WT_1 are mostly higher and those from WT_0 are mostly lower. The reverse is true for Melody Ia. The relationship between these two melodies thus involves a sharp contrast of character and interval, beneath which we find a range of subtle affinities and associations. These mutual relationships are doubtless what led the composer to imagine one of the melodies (Ia) as a variant of the other (I).

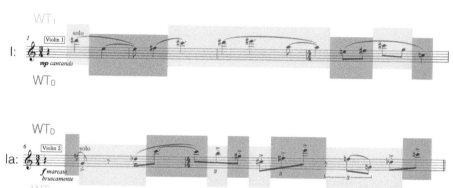

For Melodies I and II, the contrasts are more vivid, and the associations more subtle. Melody II mostly ascends by small intervals, 1s and 2s, punctuated by two large downward leaps. It often twists around on itself as it ascends—there are eight statements of a three-note motive involving 1 and 2 moving in opposite directions.

Melody 2: mostly ascends using 1 and 2
punctuated by two large downward leaps

3-note motives with 1 and 2 in opposite directions

Melody II incorporates large transposed chunks: its first eight notes are transposed up 16 semitones (T_4) and then another eight semitones (T_8), to bring it back to its starting level two octaves higher than it began.

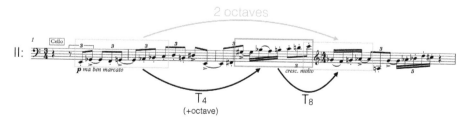

2 octaves

In its intervallic arrangement, its twisting in on itself, its motion by small increments, and its overall character (rapid notes, soft, *ben marcato*), Melody II is quite distinct from Melody I. But the two melodies have subtle affinities, including the sharing of groups of notes. Most notably, the first three notes of Melody I return as the last three notes of the first phrase of Melody II, and the dyad E–F♯, in that order, occurs at the beginning of Melody I and at the end of the first phrase of Melody II.

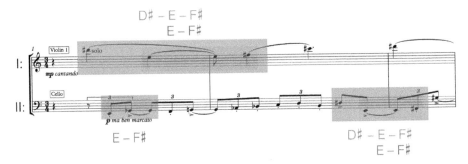

Melodies I and II also share two other features with each other (and with Melody Ia). The first is partitioning into complementary whole-tone collections. For melodies I and Ia, this partitioning is mostly by register. Melody II ascends mostly along WT$_0$, with brief detours away and back.

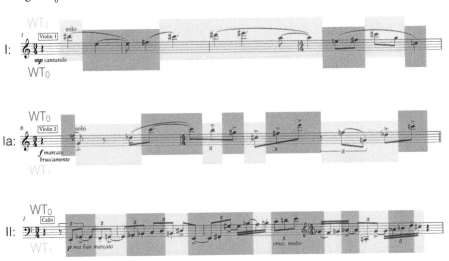

The three melodies also share an interest in inversion on a D#/E-A/B♭ axis. In Melodies I and Ia, notes are heard in close proximity to their inversional partners. In Melody II, the inversional partners tend to be balanced symmetrically in register.

Whatever their internal similarities, however, the melodies give the initial impression of being composed quite separately from each other—each melody maintains a high level of independence, seemingly virtually uncoordinated with the others. But it is possible to imagine a counterpoint that relates the vertical intervals formed between Theme I and Theme II. It is what the composer called "dissonant counterpoint"—the principal intervals are the dissonant ones (10s and 11s) while the more consonant intervals have a secondary, embellishing function.

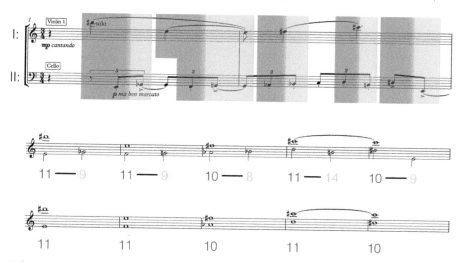

When thinking about the passage as a whole, we are probably aware first of three independent melodies, with distinctive and contrasting characters, each going its own way in its own manner, with little heed of or resemblance to the others. As we listen more carefully, however, we become aware of networks of subtle affinities and similarities that bind the melodies to each other. The cumulative effect is that of a family argument—the participants resemble each other in subtle ways, and give signs of actually listening to each other, at least some of the time.

11

Anton Webern, "Wie bin ich froh!" from *Three Songs*, Op. 25, No. 1 (1934)

This song sets a poem by Hildegarde Jone. It has a texture that is sometimes called "pointillistic"—small jabs of notes and vertiginous melodic leaps that seem to preclude any possibility of musical connection and coherence. But amid the isolated bursts of activity and sudden leaps there are subtle repetitions. For example, the poetic rhyme ("Wie bin ich froh" and "und leuchtet so") is supported by a musical rhyme: the last four notes are the same as the first four. Through it all, the music seems to shimmer with bright colors, thus resonating with a text about springtime growth.

Wie bin ich froh!
noch einmal wird mir alles grün
und leuchtet so!

How happy I am!
Once more all grows green around me
And shines so!

A rich network of musical relationships grows from the first three notes and their intervals—the musical relationships burgeon as a reflection of a text in which "Once more all grows green around me / And shines so!" The first three melody notes, G–E–D♯, present intervals <-3, +11> The same pattern of intervals occurs twice more in the melody, first transposed down five semitones, then transposed up five semitones.

The Art of Post-Tonal Analysis. Joseph N. Straus, Oxford University Press. © Joseph N. Straus 2022.
DOI: 10.1093/oso/9780197543979.003.0011

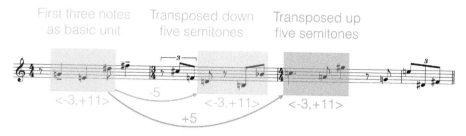

This creates both a sense of symmetrical balance and a framework for the melody: its first note, G (the first note in the first of the three motives), its lowest note B (the second note in the second of the three motives), and its highest note, G♯ (the third note in the third of the three motives). In a more abstract sense, this melodic frame has the same intervals as the three-note motive.

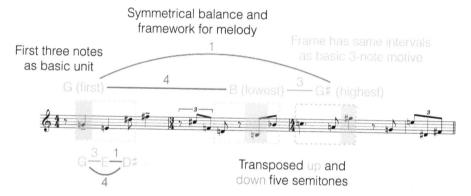

An additional, slightly varied form of the three-note motive is somewhat concealed in the melody, overlapping with the second of the three principal statements.

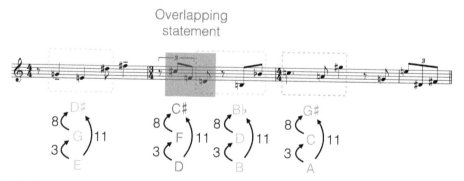

The last four notes—the ones with the G–E–D♯–F♯ rhyme—are arranged in register so that the lowest three represent yet another form of the basic three-note motive. Taken as a whole, the melody is rich in direct and varied statements of the three-note motive.

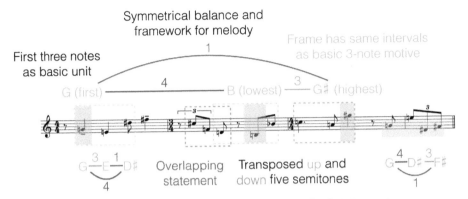

There is a great deal of obvious imitation between the vocal melody and the piano accompaniment: the central three-note motive is heard five times in a recurring rhythmic figure in the piano part.

We gain additional perspective on these and other, more subtle, imitations within and between the parts by focusing on the twelve-tone organization of the passage as a whole: the melody states one twelve-tone series; the piano part has three statements of the series.

Let's inspect these two series-forms for their segmental subsets—we are particularly interested in the set class of the three-note motive, (014): it occurs four times within the series. Every note other than F♯ in P_7 and G♯ in I_7 is a member of at least one form of this set class.

	(014)				(014)		(014)			(014)	
P7:	G	E	D♯	F♯	C♯	F	D	B	B♭	C	A	G♯
I7:	G	B♭	B	G♯	C♯	A	C	D♯	E	D	F	F♯

In addition to these intervallic similarities, four of the actual pitch-class dyads are shared between the two series forms, and these can be heard echoing back and forth within and between the parts.

Rhythmically, the piano part consists of just four recurring figures: a sixteenth-note triplet; an eighth-note dyad; a single note; and a four-note chord. The triplets always represent (014), containing intervals 1, 3, and 4. The dyads are always interval 1. The four-note chords combine two 1s or a 1 and a 3. The single notes combine with nearby vocal melody notes to create additional forms of (014). In all of these ways, the intervals of the initial melodic trichord resonate throughout the passage.

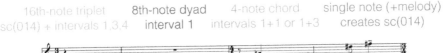

12

Milton Babbitt, "The Widow's Lament in Springtime" (1951)

This work, a setting of a poem by William Carlos Williams, is composed in four distinct lines: the vocal melody plus three contrapuntal melodies in the piano: high, middle, and low.

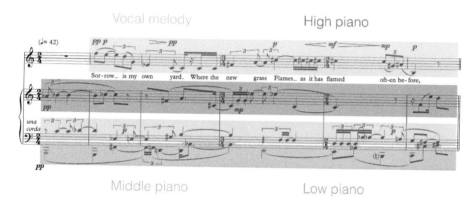

The vocal melody is roughly in three parts, corresponding to three distinct moments in the text. First, the text expresses grief ("Sorrow is my own yard"), and the music invokes three traditionally sorrowful musical gestures: a descending semitone (the traditional sighing motive); a minor triad (C minor); and a relentlessly descending contour. Second, the music sparks upward, evoking flamelike quality of the burgeoning of spring ("Where the new grass Flames, as it has flamed"). Finally, the music subsides with a reference to past happiness, now lost ("often before").

This roughly symmetrical arrangement of melodic gestures is confirmed in the intervals and pitches of the melody. It contains all twelve notes, arranged so that each of the eleven ordered pitch-class intervals occurs once: one 1, one 2, one 3, and so on, up to 11. The intervals are arranged symmetrically: the first interval, 11,

The Art of Post-Tonal Analysis. Joseph N. Straus, Oxford University Press. © Joseph N. Straus 2022.
DOI: 10.1093/oso/9780197543979.003.0012

is the complement of the last interval, 1; the second interval, 10, is the complement of the second-to-last interval, 2; and so on. The symmetry is also reflected in the pitches: the last six notes are related to the first six notes by T_6, in reverse order.

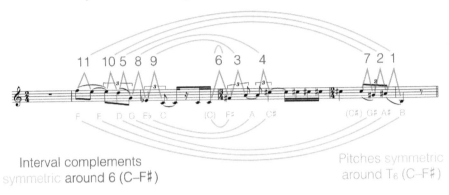

Symmetrical arrangement of intervals and pitches

Interval complements symmetric around 6 (C–F♯)

Pitches symmetric around T_6 (C–F♯)

The twelve-note melody is articulated into two hexachords and four trichords. The hexachords are complementary members of set-class (023457). The trichords are either (013) or (037), the set-class of the major or minor triad.

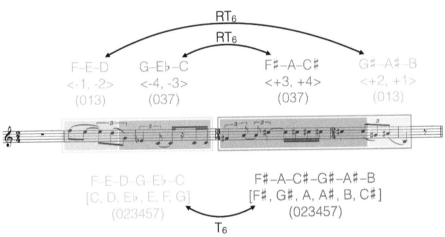

All four lines are composed in just this way: the first six notes are related to the last six at T_6 in reverse order; both hexachords are members of (023457). The top two lines have the same trichords in reverse order; so do the bottom two. The result is a densely interwoven musical texture, with intense imitation of a small number of three-note motives.

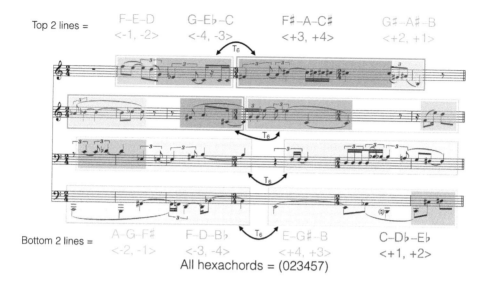

Top 2 lines =

F–E–D	G–E♭–C	F♯–A–C♯	G♯–A♯–B
<-1, -2>	<-4, -3>	<+3, +4>	<+2, +1>

Bottom 2 lines =

A–G–F♯	F–D–B♭	E–G♯–B	C–D♭–E♭
<-2, -1>	<-3, -4>	<+4, +3>	<+1, +2>

All hexachords = (023457)

In each of the four sections of the passage, we find an aggregate of all twelve notes formed between the lines. Each line contributes one trichord to these vertical aggregates, within which the trichords are all of the same type, either (013) or (037). And the trichords are arranged in their four possible intervallic orderings: within a vertical aggregate, no two trichords share the same intervallic ordering. The music thus explores simultaneously an extreme of unification (all trichords within an aggregate are of the same type) and an extreme of variety (no two trichords have the same arrangement of intervals).

One trichord per line, same type; all four intervallic orderings

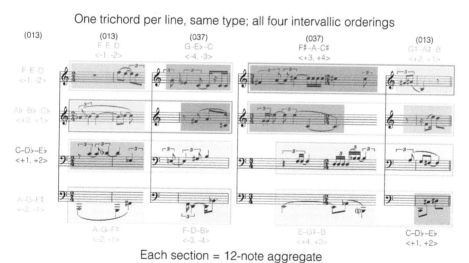

Each section = 12-note aggregate

Everything we have discussed so far—about aggregates, hexachords, trichords, and intervals within the lines—is an aspect of the twelve-tone design for the piece. But the passage is also rich in "associative harmony," that is, groupings of notes that do not fall out of the twelve-tone design but result rather from free compositional choices. Consider, for example, the way the song begins. Babbitt knows in advance, from the twelve-tone design, that the lowest line will start on A and the top line in the piano will start on A♭. But the decision to have those two notes sound simultaneously, and without any other notes sounding, is a free compositional choice. On what basis does Babbitt make a choice like that? Well, the interval between those notes is a semitone, and a semitone is one of the intervals in the melodic (013) that all four lines are presenting linearly.

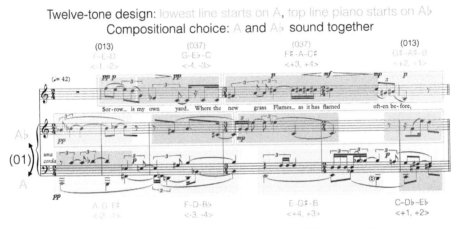

Twelve-tone design: lowest line starts on A, top line piano starts on A♭
Compositional choice: A and A♭ sound together

A♭–A is a semitone (01), part of melodic (013) in every line twice

In this passage, it is relatively rare that two notes are attacked at the same time, as they are on the downbeat of the first measure. These simultaneously attacked dyads often involve the intervals of the initial (013), namely 1, 2, and 3. The cumulative result is a music that simultaneously explores maximum concentration and maximum variety.

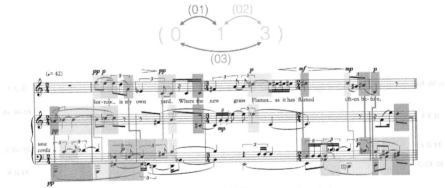

Melodic (013) in every line twice

13

Luigi Dallapiccola, "Die Sonne kommt!" from *Goethe Lieder*, No. 2 (1953)

This is a twelve-tone piece, based on a pair of inversionally related series and their retrogrades.

The vocal line moves forward through $P_{G\#}$ and I_A, then retraces its steps in retrograde. The retrograde is strict as to both pitch and rhythm. The clarinet melody repeats the first half of the vocal melody, again strictly as to both pitch and rhythm. The result is a canon at the unison between the parts. In the second half of the piece, the vocal and clarinet melodies are retrogrades of each other.

The Art of Post-Tonal Analysis. Joseph N. Straus, Oxford University Press. © Joseph N. Straus 2022.
DOI: 10.1093/oso/9780197543979.003.0013

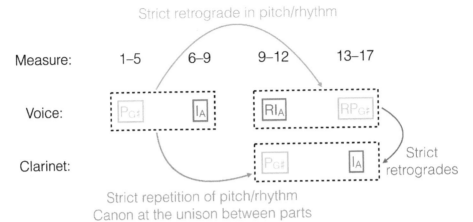

There is considerable redundancy among the trichords of the series, with two segments representing (012), (025), and (016).

Trichords made of (012), (025), and (016)

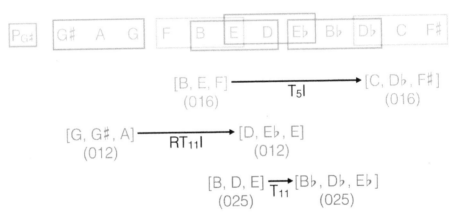

In the music, the recurrence of (016) is made particularly prominent by its position at the end of the two six-note phrases.

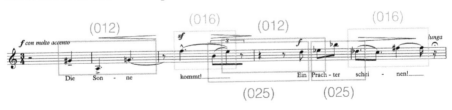

Within $P_{G\sharp}$, these two (016) are related at T_5I. As a result, they remain invariant in I_A, the T_5I-related series form. Not only are these trichords invariant between the two forms, but so are two additional dyads: G#–A and Eb–D. The invariance is so extensive that the two series forms are practically variations of each other.

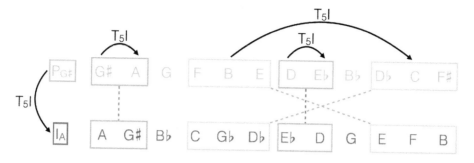

Invariant between P_G♯ and I_a:
trichords [B, E, F] and [C, D♭, F♯]
dyads: [G♯, A] and [D, E♭]

In the music, there is thus constant echo and imitation both within and between the parts. This is most evident in the second half of the song, where the two series forms are heard together.

One consequence of this intense invariance is that the same hexachords that are found within the two series are also found between them, drawing three notes from one series and three from the other.

The meaning of the poem is richly expressed in these relationships within and between series. The basis of the poem is a paradoxical, enigmatic contact between the sun and the moon: as radically different as they are, they nonetheless find a way to embrace. In Dallapiccola's setting, $P_{G\sharp}$ is associated with the sun (it sets the first line of text: "The sun comes! A shining splendor!") and I_A with the moon (it sets the second line of text: "The crescent moon embraces it"). In the second half of the song, the music enacts the embrace of the two parts, heightening their similarities and joining them in the mutual creation of hexachords they also possess individually.

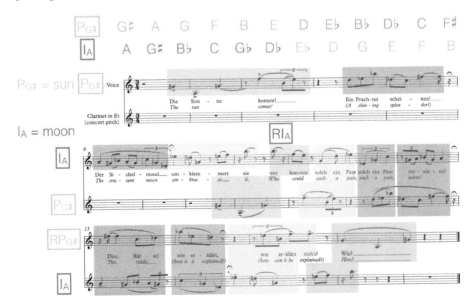

14

Igor Stravinsky, "Music to Hear," from *Three Shakespeare Songs*, No. 2 (1953)

This song, a setting of a sonnet by Shakespeare, is scored for mezzo-soprano, flute, clarinet, and viola (the instrumental introduction is the passage we will be studying here). It was written in the early years of Stravinsky's new interest in serial and twelve-tone composition. The passage presents two contrasting melodies. The melody in the flute is smooth and lyrical, although with some large leaps. At the same time, the clarinet and viola share a contrasting melody, played mostly staccato, and with the line tossed rapidly back and forth between the instruments.

Melody 1: flute, smooth and lyrical, some large leaps

Melody 2: contrasting staccato, tossed between instruments

The first four notes in the flute melody, B–G–A–B♭, function as a referential series for the melody and for most of the rest of the song. It opens up a space between B and G, and then fills that space partly in. Only the A♭ is missing within the span.

The Art of Post-Tonal Analysis. Joseph N. Straus, Oxford University Press. © Joseph N. Straus 2022.
DOI: 10.1093/oso/9780197543979.003.0014

P_B: basic series for entire song

Opens space
from B to G

< 8,   2,   1 >

Partially fills
in the space

Only A♭ is missing

Starting at the end of measure 3, we hear the same four notes, in the same order, and therefore with the same intervals.

Same four notes in the same order

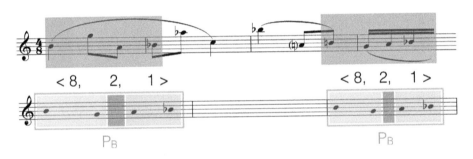

In between the two statement of the four-note series we find a contrasting four-note series, related to them by inversion. Each interval in the original series <8, 2, 1> is replaced, in order, by its complement mod 12 <4, 10, 11>. That's the definition of inversion: what goes up by some amount in one goes down by the same amount in the other, and vice versa.

Contrasting four-note series

Original intervals **replaced by** complement

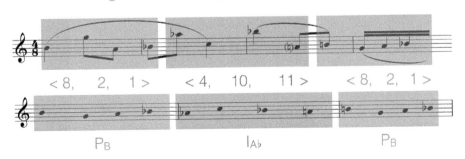

There are at least three reasons why Stravinsky may have chosen this particular inversion, the one that starts on A♭. First, the A♭ fills in the gap within the original series. The inversion starting on A♭ then creates its own gap. Its missing B is filled in when the first four notes return.

Why I$_{A♭}$?

Gap in P$_B$ filled by I$_{A♭}$; gap in I$_{A♭}$ filled by P$_B$

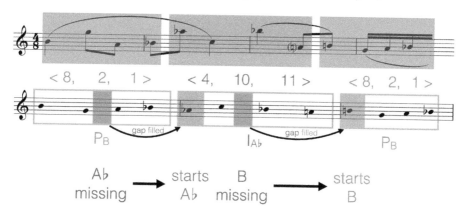

Second, taken together, the two four-note series chromatically fill the span between G and C: G–A♭–A–B♭–B–C. The relationship between G and C is the basis for the accompanying line, as we will see.

Why I$_{A♭}$?

P$_B$ and I$_{A♭}$ fill span between G and C (basis for accompaniment)

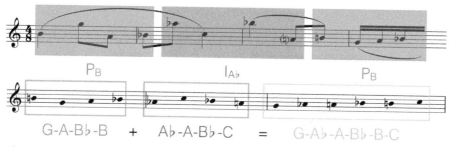

G-A-B♭-B   +   A♭-A-B♭-C   =   G-A♭-A-B♭-B-C

Third, the two series forms are related by the inversion that balances G against C. That's another hint of the importance of the relationship between these tones. Note that this same inversion also exchanges A and B♭: the last two notes of the original series return, in reverse order, as the last two notes of the inversion. Performing that inversion twice takes us back to our starting point.

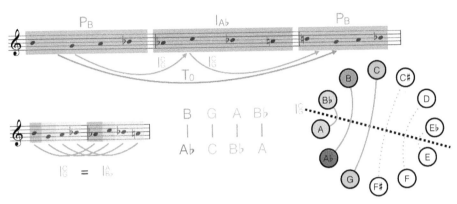

Why $I_{A\flat}$?

Inversion **balances** B/A♭, G/C, and A/B♭

The second half of the melody is organized in a very similar fashion. Again, there are twelve notes, where the first four and the last four are the same. In between, we have a four-note series form related to these by inversion.

Second half of melody organized similarly to first:

Begins and ends with same four notes in the same order

Contrasting four-note series

Original intervals **replaced by** complement

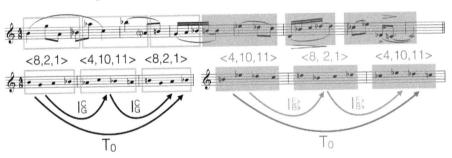

Looking at the melody as a whole, we note that the first twelve notes and the last twelve notes are related by inversion around B. Everything the first twelve notes do above B, the second twelve do below B, and vice versa. Inversional symmetry thus plays a role within each half of the melody and between its halves as well. If we think of the first half of the melody as moving down a semitone from B, the first note, to B♭, the twelfth note, we can think of the second half of the melody as moving up a semitone from B, its first note, to C, the last note. This sense of directed motion toward C is also important for the accompanying part, as we will see.

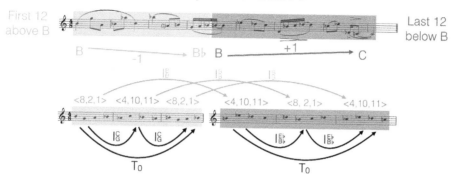

The actual music—its rhythm, and phrasing, and articulation—frequently contradicts the serial design's grouping into four-note units. Just considering the phrasing slurs, we have a group of six, a group of three, a group of four (but the wrong four), a group of three, and only at the very end do we get two phrase groups that actually coincide with the four-note serial design.

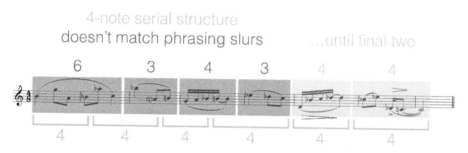

For the sake of comparison, I offer a horrible hypothetical recomposition of Stravinsky's melody. My horrible version aligns with the four-note serial plan in rhythm and register, and highlights by contrast the extent to which Stravinksy's melody obscures it, with its phrasing and especially its octave displacements and disjunct contour. Stravinsky's surface conceals rather than reveals the music's inner organization, and that sort of tense relationship among the structural levels is a persistent feature of his music, and of musical modernism generally: a feature, not a bug. The serial scheme provides an underlying regularity that the melodic surface plays with and against.

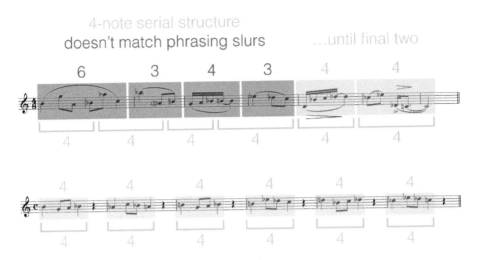

The music not only conceals its four-note serial organization, but it also seems to evoke and contradict a simple tonal prototype in C major, with a four-measure antecedent phrase and a four-measure consequent phrase. Stravinsky's melody toys with this implicit conventional prototype, rushing ahead or holding back, and thus deforming the regularities and symmetries of the prototype.

Let's turn now to the accompanying line, shared by clarinet and viola. Like the flute melody, this line is quite disjunct in contour, with lots of big leaps, and is further broken up by the frequent changes of instrumental timbre. But underlying that melodic activity is something very regular and systematic: the line just trots up and down the first five notes of a C major scale. It is possible to think of that in serial terms, as the presentation and transformation of a five-note series, C–D–E–F–G. We could think of the ascending and descending patterns as related by retrograde, but I think it makes more sense to think of them as related by (diatonic) inversion: they are mirror images of each other within the C-G frame.

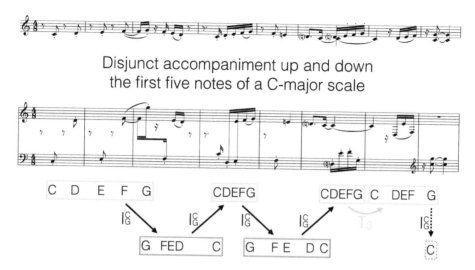

Disjunct accompaniment up and down
the first five notes of a C-major scale

A concern with inversion around $\begin{smallmatrix}C\\G\end{smallmatrix}$ is something the two melodies share. The flute melody has six statements of its chromatic four-note series; the accompanying line has six statements of its diatonic five-note series. The series in the flute melody alternate original and inverted presentations, and the first two statements are related by the inversion that exchanges C and G. The series in the accompanying line also alternate presentations, ascending and descending, and in a diatonic sense, they can also be understood as related by the inversion that exchanges C and G.

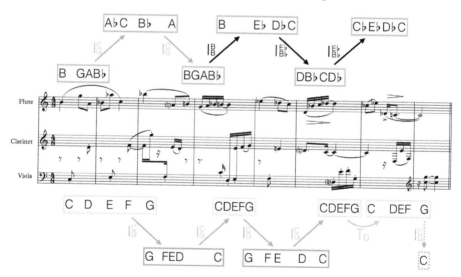

The two contrasting melodies also share a common interest in the space between C and G and in directing their motion toward C. The flute melody fills that space chromatically in its first three series statements: G–A♭–A–B♭–B–C. The accompanying line fills that space diatonically again and again: C–D–E–F–G. In the final measure, we hear that perfect fifth all alone as a cadential sonority. The flute melody directs its motion toward its final C by its large-scale inversional plan: the first half of the melody descends from B to B♭; the second half ascends from B to

C. The accompanying line directs its motion toward C in its final descent through the diatonic fifth from G to C. We have a passage that pits two opposing lines against each other. At first glance, the lines seem entirely different from each other: one is built on a four-note chromatic series; the other simply trots up and down the first five notes of a C major scale. But gradually we become aware that the lines have a good deal in common: not only do they both consist of six statements of an underlying series, but they are both concerned with the space between C and G, and with C as a shared cadential goal. In the cadential perfect fifth, C-G, the lines seem to come together in mutual harmony.

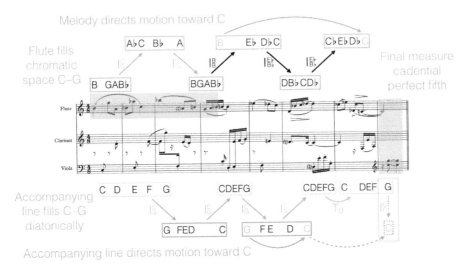

In this way, this song makes a wonderful musical analogue for the Shakespeare sonnet that is its text. In this poem, the presumptively male narrator encourages his presumptively male friend to get married. He argues that a man and a woman are like two sounding strings on an instrument—they are different, but if properly tuned to each other, beautiful sounds can result. It would be hard to imagine a more apt musical realization of that idea, with two contrasting melodies merging in "the true concord of well-tuned sounds."

15

Louise Talma, "La Corona," from
Holy Sonnets (1955)

This is a choral setting of one of John Donne's Holy Sonnets, poetic hymns of praise to God. In this stanza, the poet contrasts his own poor, ephemeral art ("Weaved in my low devout melancholy") with the inexhaustible and immutable goodness of God ("All changing unchanged Ancient of days"). In response, the composer offers two contrasting kinds of music: chords (associated with God) and canons (associated with the human artistic creation).

Deign at my hands this crown of prayer and praise,
Weaved in my low devout melancholy,

The Art of Post-Tonal Analysis. Joseph N. Straus, Oxford University Press. © Joseph N. Straus 2022.
DOI: 10.1093/oso/9780197543979.003.0015

Chords

Canons

Chords

Thou which of good hast, yea art treasury,
All changing unchanged Ancient of days.

We'll start by looking at the canons, those traditional manifestations of composerly craft. They are based on a twelve-note series, but an unusual one: it omits some notes (E, F, B) and has two occurrences of others (D♭, E♭, A♭). It features the perfect fourth/fifth (5/7); every note other than A and D is connected by that interval to at least one adjacent note.

Canon: unusual 12-note series

Features perfect 4th/5th (5/7)

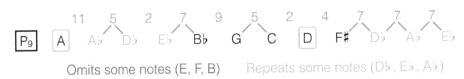

Omits some notes (E, F, B)   Repeats some notes (D♭, E♭, A♭)

In addition to its intervals, the series features three types of tetrachords that are important units in the piece, both melodically and harmonically.

Series features three important tetrachords

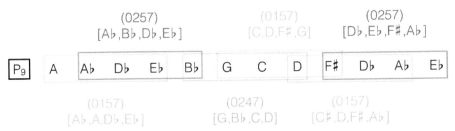

In the canonic passages, every note is accounted for in relation to a small number of transpositions of this series. In the first of the two canonic passages, a two-voice canon in soprano and tenor, sharing P_9, shifts to alto and bass, sharing P_5. Because the rhythmic interval between the voices in this slightly inexact canon is so small (one or two quarter notes), the collections of notes (especially dyads and tetrachords) formed between the voices are precisely those formed within each voice. For example, in measures 7–8, we hear B♭-G in the soprano, then the same interval formed between soprano and tenor, and then the same interval again within the tenor. The same is true of the tetrachords: we hear them both within and between the parts. For example, the first four notes of P_9 in the soprano, A–A♭–D♭–E♭, are heard again between the parts when the tenor enters, and then once again within the tenor part. This interweaving of notes within and between the parts nicely reflects the poem, which describes itself as "weaved in my low devout melancholy."

The second canon is a four-voice canon: the soprano leads with the first eight notes of RP_{11}, followed by the tenor (just as in the first canon), the bass, and the alto. Once again, the intervals and larger groupings within the melodies recur as harmonies between the parts—a musical interweaving. At the end of the passage, the texture blends over into chordal homophony, and the chord in measure 19 is a segment of P_{11}: notes 5–8. They represent a form of (0247), which is the basis for all of the chordal passages. In a vivid musical representation of the text, this harmony, (0247) is offered up by the human artist—the musical weaver—to the "all changing, unchanged" God.

The chordal passages are a musical "crown of prayer and praise" to the eternal "Ancient of days." The first of the two chordal passages can be parsed into four chords representing three forms of (0247) (if we exclude the first E♭ in the bass and the A♭ in the alto). The first chord is revoiced, then progresses via I_7 (the voice leading reflects the inversion exactly) and T_2 to its destination.

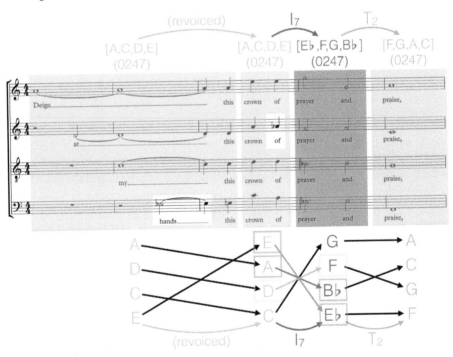

The harmony (0247) can be thought of as a major triad with added ninth or a minor triad with added fourth. If we extract the triads embedded within the (0247)s in this passage, we find a progression that starts on A minor, moves to E♭ major (via a transformation I am calling OCTPOLE: major and minor triads with tritone-related roots, falling within an octatonic collection), and then, via T_2, to F major. The initial A minor moves to the concluding F major via L. These harmonic moves have two seemingly contradictory qualities. They are quite distant in traditional tonal terms: no single key contains all three of them, and the harmonic relationship between A minor and E♭ major is particularly remote. But the voice leading intervals that connect them are small. The effect of chords that are remote harmonically but close in voice-leading distance has sometimes been thought of as uncanny—simultaneously strange and distant, yet close at hand and deeply familiar. In this context, a subtle musical representation of a God who is both remote and yet intimately close to us.

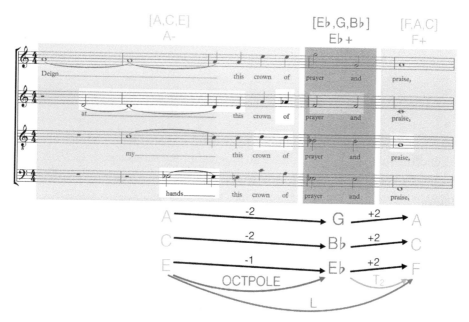

The canons, representing the poetic weaver, are based on the twelve-tone series. The chords, representing the unchanging God, are based on (0247) chords and their embedded triads. How do canons and chords, human and divine, relate to each other? First, the type of harmony for all of the chords, (0247), is a segment of the series, situated right at its center.

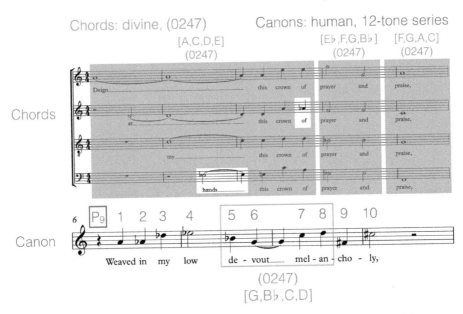

Second, the vocal parts within the chord progression are series segments. Most conspicuously, the four notes of the tenor part, [G, B♭, C, D], are precisely the four notes found in the middle of P_9, which forms the canonic subject.

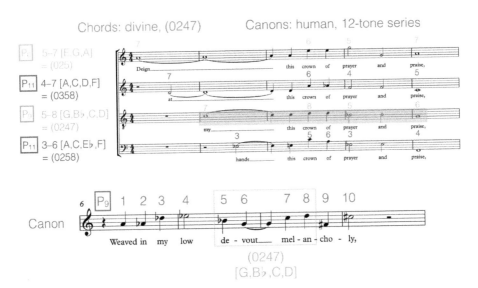

The second progression of chords, like the first, is engaged with (0247), but also brings in (0157), another tetrachordal subset-type found in the series. These two chords can be understood as related by fuzzy-T_{-4}.

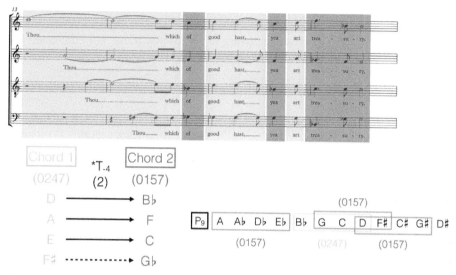

The upper three voices enact fuzzy-T_{-4} in a direct way: the soprano descends D–B♭; the alto descends A–F; the tenor descends E–C. The soprano part offers yet another form of (0247).

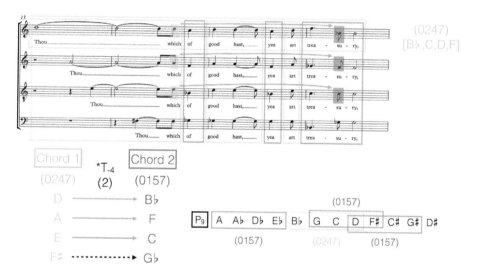

The third and final progression consists of just two chords, both members of (0247). (0247) is embedded in the series and the canons are derived from it. These canons, creations of human artistic craft, offer up their (0247) as the principal source of chordal harmony, just as the poet offers up a hymn of praise to God. If we imagine these chords as a major or minor triad plus one extra note, we can hear that they are hexatonic poles—harmonically distant in traditional terms but connected by semitonal voice leading. The relationship is uncanny in its description of a God simultaneously high above and close within.

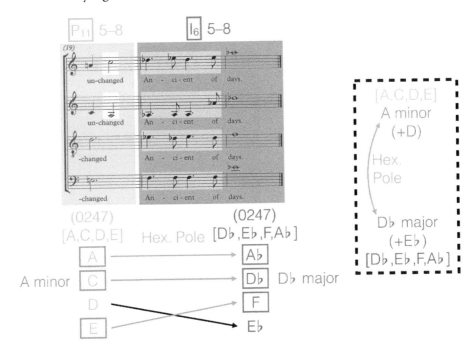

16

Hale Smith, *Three Brevities for Solo Flute*, No. 2 (1969)

This piece for solo flute begins with an eighteen-note musical idea divided into four gesturally and intervallically distinct components, labeled W, X, Y, and Z. W is hexatonic; X is chromatic; Y is octatonic; Z, which operates as a sort of tag to the phrase as a whole, combines elements of W, X, and Y.

18-note musical idea divided into 4 segments

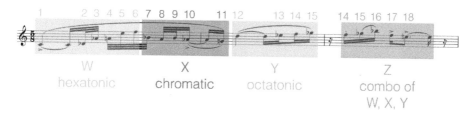

The piece as a whole explores the contrasts and affinities between these four components, as well as the possibilities of combining them into larger shapes.

W is an upward rocket, rapidly ascending through alternating semitones and perfect fifths. It traverses a complete 1–7 cycle—the next note in the cycle would be a return to C. Taken as a whole, W states a complete hexatonic collection, HEX_{01}: C-D♭-E-F-A♭-A. Each of its segmental trichords is a member of (015), and these are

The Art of Post-Tonal Analysis. Joseph N. Straus, Oxford University Press. © Joseph N. Straus 2022.
DOI: 10.1093/oso/9780197543979.003.0016

linked into an RI-chain. From the point of view of transpositional combination, W can be thought of as three semitones related by T_4/T_8.

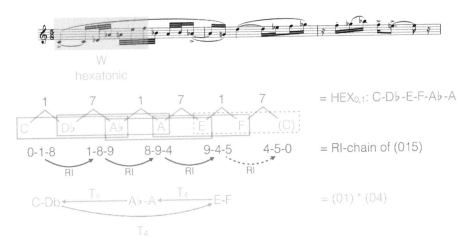

If W is an upward rocket, X puts the brakes on, moving slowly within a narrow compass from B♭ down to G. Omitting the repeated B♭, it describes a descending 1-cycle. Taken as a whole, X states a form of the chromatic tetrachord, (0123): G-A♭-A-B♭. Each of its segmental trichords is a member of (012), and these are linked into an RI-chain. From the point of view of transpositional combination, X can be thought of as two semitones related by T_2/T_{10}. In short, X does in a chromatic space what W does in a hexatonic space.

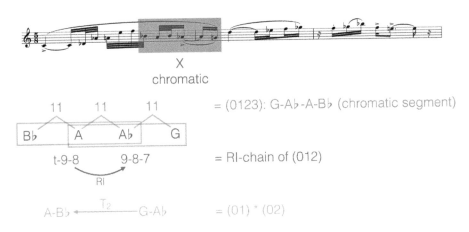

If W is hexatonic and X is chromatic, Y is octatonic. Like W, Y ascends through a compound interval cycle, alternating 1 and 2. It forms a segment of an octatonic scale, (0134). It embeds two forms of (013), arranged as an RI-chain. It can be thought of as two semitones related by T_3.

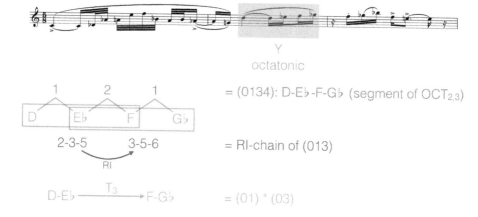

Z lacks the cyclic and transpositional aspects of W, X, and Y, but it recalls each of them collectionally: (015) from W; (012) from X; and the F–G♭ semitone from Y.

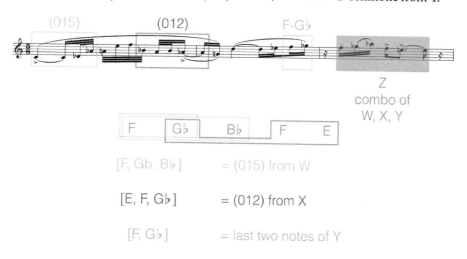

In addition, the last three notes of Z, B♭–F–E, form (016), which is found along with (015) at the boundaries between the components. The opening eighteen notes thus form a richly integrated and unified idea, composed of four distinct components that nonetheless are formed in similar ways, share internal features, and are joined together by set-types they contain.

(016) and (015) found at boundaries of phrase and segments

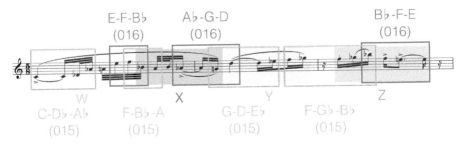

The opening eighteen-note idea resonates through the rest of the piece, sometimes in its entirety, and sometimes just its individual components. Indeed, one can do something of an "eighteen-count" of the movement, treating the first eighteen notes as a series (a line of pitch classes, more or less fixed in order, but free as to octave position).

With these clear landmarks in place, it is possible to see the whole piece as a series of statements of W–X–Y–Z. W has an initiating function, and its appearances divide the piece into five sections, with the final section petering out into fragmented and truncated statements of the four components. In many cases, these components are fragmented, reordered, reduced in scope to one or two notes, but still recognizable. Having based the piece on four contrasting components, the composer seems particularly interested in exploring the boundaries between them and the common elements they share. By the end, the references have been reduced to single tones, and the movement ends with the dyad G-D, at the boundary between X and Y.

17

Elisabeth Lutyens, *Two Bagatelles*, Op. 48, No. 1 (1962)

This twelve-tone piece uses only three different forms of its series: P_6 (heard four times), RP_7, and I_5.

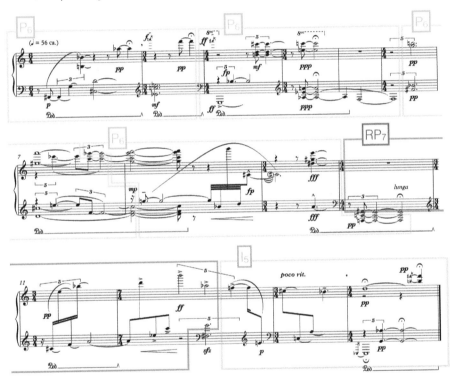

The two hexachords of the series are complementary, of course, but they are not related by transposition or inversion. They are, however, related by M5—that's the so-called "circle of fourths transformation," which turns semitones into perfect fourths, and vice versa. The first hexachord can be thought of as two (037) related at T_1. In the second hexachord, the (037) become (014): both sets contain intervals 3 and 4, and the 5 within (037) has become the 1 within (014). At the same time, the T_1 that connects the (037) in the first hexachord has become the T_5 that connects the (014) in the second hexachord.

The Art of Post-Tonal Analysis. Joseph N. Straus, Oxford University Press. © Joseph N. Straus 2022.
DOI: 10.1093/oso/9780197543979.003.0017

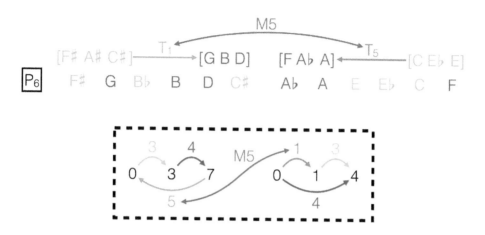

This way of dividing up the series into hexachords and the hexachords into T-related trichords is frequently overt throughout the piece, especially at the beginning and end.

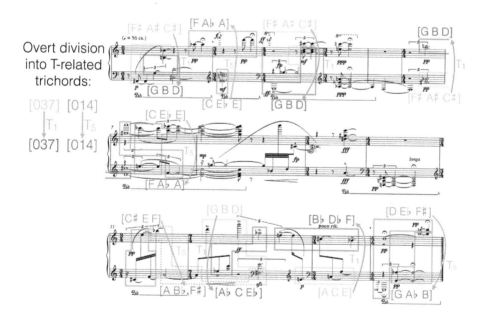

There is a large-scale oscillation between the (037)-dominated hexachord and the (014)-dominated hexachord. But both of these trichords have an independent life in the piece, penetrating into space nominally occupied by the complementary hexachord. The opening phrase, for example, can be interpreted as a network either of (037) or (014). Let's consider it first as a network of (014). The trichords are connected locally by common-tone preserving contextual inversions, arranged as an RI-chain. The intervals of transposition that connect the (014) are those belonging to (037): 3, 4, and 7.

Network of (014) connected by contextual inversion and transposition

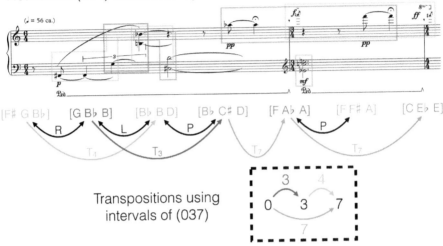

Looking at the passage again, this time as a network of (037), we find that the trichords are again connected locally by common-tone preserving contextual inversions, arranged as an RI-chain. Just as the (014) were connected by the intervals of (037), the (037) are connected by the intervals of (014): 1, 3, and 4.

Network of (037) connected by contextual inversion and transposition

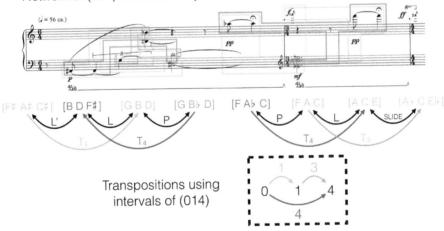

We've considered the hexachords and trichords. Now let's go back to the series and consider individual tones and intervals. The three series forms share common segments of various lengths. They all also begin and end on F, G♯, or G.

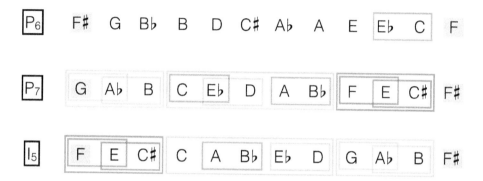

These first and last tones of each series are often salient in the music especially at the beginnings and endings of phrases. Furthermore, the only note in the piece not clearly accounted for as part of one of these series is the *sf* F♯ in measure twelve.

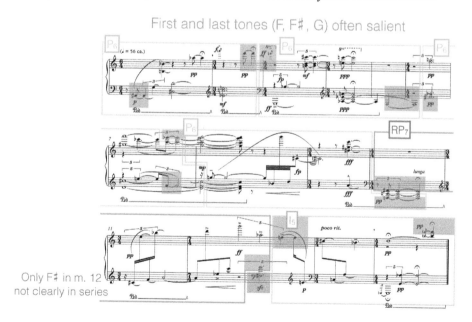

These boundary tones—F, F#, and G—not only mark the phrases of the piece, but they are often heard in close proximity to each other, especially F-F# and F#-G. These are only the most prominent of a network of semitones that permeate the piece. Within the series, every note other than C is connected by semitone to an adjacent note, and the semitones are connected only by 3/9 or 5/7.

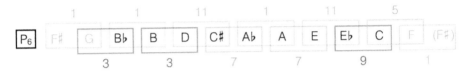

The semitones are prominent in the music and can be gathered into networks in which a semitone (01) is transposed by the intervals of a consonant triad (037). This arises because the first hexachord of the series, like any member of (013478), can be divided into two consonant triads related at T_1. Passages based on it can be thought in two complementary ways, either as two (037)s transposed by semitone (a relationship we already discussed) or as three semitones transposed by the intervals of (037), namely T_3, T_4, and T_7.

First hexachord divides into two triads (037) related at T_1
or three semitones related at intervals of (037): T_3, T_4, T_7

P_6 [F# A# C#] $\xrightarrow{\ T_1\ }$ [G B D]   [F#,G] [Bb,B] [C#,D]
F# G Bb B D C#

I_5 [A C E] $\xrightarrow{\ T_1\ }$ [Bb Db F]   [E,F] [C,C#] [A,Bb]
F E C# C A Bb

P_7 [G B D] $\xrightarrow{\ T_1\ }$ [Ab C Eb]   [D,Eb] [B,C] [G,Ab]
G Ab B C Eb D

The semitones in the music can be gathered into networks in which they are transposed by the intervals of a consonant triad (037): T_3, T_4, and T_7. Previously, we considered how the twelve-tone series is divided into hexachords, and hexachords into trichords, and trichords into intervals. Now we get a hint of the process in reverse, as intervals combine to form trichords and hexachords, and ultimately twelve-tone aggregates.

Prominent semitones in networks transposed by intervals of consonant triad

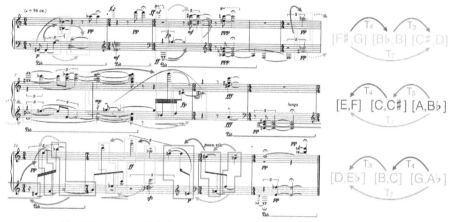

First hexachord divides into three semitones related at T_3, T_4, T_7

18

Igor Stravinsky, *Fanfare for a New Theatre* (1964)

This fanfare for two trumpets was composed to commemorate the opening of the newly constructed Lincoln Center in New York City. In its first performance, the two trumpet players were positioned on opposite sides of the balcony of what was then called the New York State Theater. It has many of the qualities of a traditional celebratory fanfare, including rapid repeated notes, antiphonal imitation between the parts, and virtuosic display.

The piece is based on what for Stravinsky was a standard quartet of series forms: a Prime and an Inversion starting on the same note (in this case, A♯) plus the Retrograde and its inversion (IR) starting on the same note (in this case, G). To this quartet, Stravinsky adjoins the retrograde of the inversion (RI).

The Art of Post-Tonal Analysis. Joseph N. Straus, Oxford University Press. © Joseph N. Straus 2022.
DOI: 10.1093/oso/9780197543979.003.0018

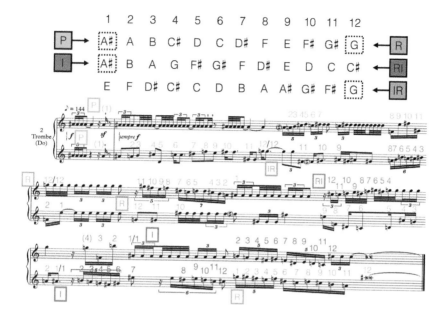

The twelve-tone series can be thought of as generated from its first three notes, A♯–A–B. If these are taken as a three-note series, the remaining discrete trichords and one additional trichord, nestled across the trichordal boundary, are forms of it, related by inversion or retrograde-inversion.

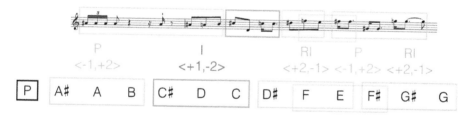

Series generated from first three notes

Because all four discrete trichords are members of a single set-class, (012), we find an extraordinary degree of invariance among the series forms. If we label the four trichords of P as W, X, Y, and Z, we find that the remaining series forms have the same four trichords (in content, not necessarily in the order of the notes).

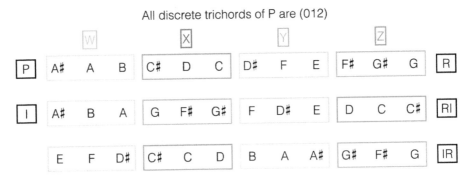

All discrete trichords of P are (012)

All rows have same four trichord content (W, X, Y, and Z)

The entire piece can be parsed into statements of these four trichords. The result is a constant sense of imitation between the parts.

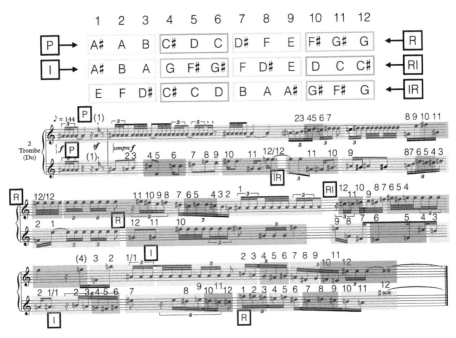

At the ending of the piece, for example, the two series forms (R and I) are related by retrograde-inversion. But the staggered disposition of trichords that are invariant between the lines produces a seemingly canonic effect. Throughout the piece, the lines simultaneously contrast serially and are virtually identified with each other motivically.

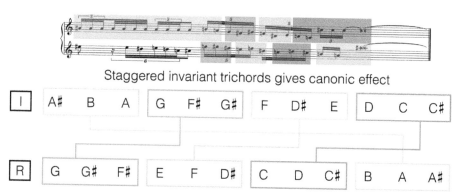

Staggered invariant trichords gives canonic effect

I	A♯	B	A	G	F♯	G♯	F	D♯	E	D	C	C♯

R	G	G♯	F♯	E	F	D♯	C	D	C♯	B	A	A♯

The trichords combine to create forms of the chromatic hexachord (012345).

Trichords combine to create chromatic hexachords

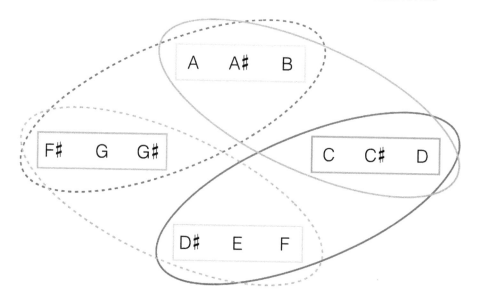

Taking again the ending of the piece, we find these chromatic hexachords both within and between the lines.

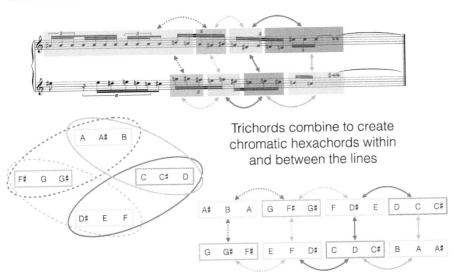

Trichords combine to create chromatic hexachords within and between the lines

Amid this highly chromatic serial and motivic activity, the piece maintains a consistent sense of centricity on A♯. It is the first note and (supported consonantly by C♯) the last note of the piece. It is heard more often and longer than any other note. It often occurs at phrase boundaries, both beginnings and endings. It provides a focus—a point of departure and return—for the motivic activity.

Consistent sense of A♯ centricity

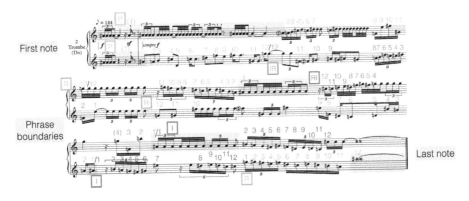

19

Igor Stravinsky, "Exaudi," from
Requiem Canticles (1966)

Requiem Canticles was Stravinsky's last major composition, written when he was 85 years old. The music is very sparsely scored, and it is presented here in a short score, which omits instrumental doubling of the vocal parts. It has a text from the traditional Latin Requiem Mass, and it is arranged in five distinct phrases.

Phase 1:
Harp Melody,
Big Chord,
Brief Chorale

Phase 2:
Harp Melody,
Big Chord,
Interjections,
Big Chord

Phase 3:
Vocal Chorale,
Interjections

Phase 4:
Vocal Chorale

Phase 5:
Instr. Chorale
with Big Chords

Exaudi, orationem meam   Hear my prayer
Ad te, omnis caro veniet   All flesh shall come before you

The first phrase consists of three distinct bits: a six-note harp melody; a six-note chord, and a brief vocal trio, setting the first line of the text.

Phrase in three parts:

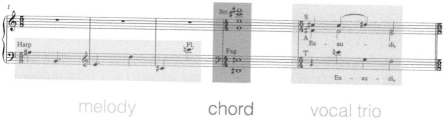

melody   chord   vocal trio

Motivically, both within and between the bits, we find a consistent interest in (013), expressed either as a 1 and a 2 moving in the same direction, or as a 2 and a 3 moving in opposite directions. E–C♯–D♯, for example, is prominent in both halves of the passage.

The Art of Post-Tonal Analysis. Joseph N. Straus, Oxford University Press. © Joseph N. Straus 2022.
DOI: 10.1093/oso/9780197543979.003.0019

(013) consistent interest throughout phrase

E-C♯-D♯ is <-3,+2>   B-D-C is <+3,-2>   E-G-F is <+3,-2>

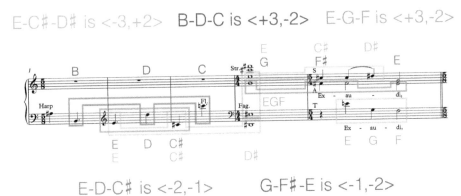

E-D-C♯ is <-2,-1>   G-F♯-E is <-1,-2>

Phrase in three parts: melody, chord, vocal trio

This piece (like a lot of Stravinsky's late music) is based on rotational arrays. A form of the twelve-tone series, in this case the retrograde (R) form, is laid across the top (Row I), then each of its hexachords is rotated and transposed, independently, to begin on the same first note: A-sharp for the six rows of the R^A-array and C for the six rows of the R^B array. In this musical passage, the harp melody states Row II of the R^A array while the chord in m. 4 and the choral passage in m. 5 both realize Row I of the R^B array.

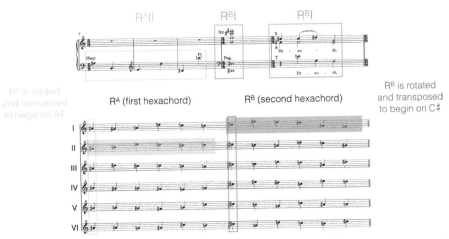

The two series-derived hexachords of the passage are related by inversion around the C♯ and E they share. That underlying inversion is at least partially suggested by the registral arrangement of the notes: the highest two notes of the harp melody are inverted onto the lowest two notes of the chord; the middle three notes of the harp melody (forming a diminished triad) become the middle three notes of the chord; the lowest harp note maps onto the highest note of the chord. Inversional symmetry plays an important role in this music, giving the music a sense of self-contained harmonious balance.

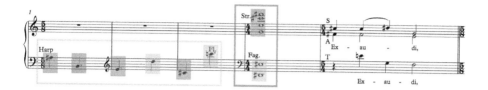

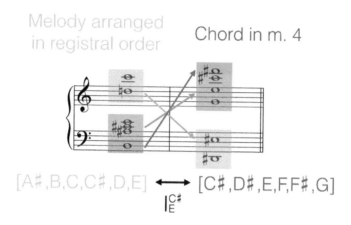

Melody arranged in registral order   Chord in m. 4

[A♯,B,C,C♯,D,E] ⟷ [C♯,D♯,E,F,F♯,G]

C♯
E

The second block begins like the first block, with a harp melody, but it continues differently: instrumental chords with the singing voices silent. The music is again based on the rows of the R-array. The first two hexachords, from R^A, are related by transposition. Both are related to the third hexachord, from R^B, by inversion. The high C in m. 8 is shared by R^AI and R^AII. The linear order of R^BIII is reflected in the registral order (lowest to highest) of the concluding chord: C♯-C-E-D-A♯-D♯.

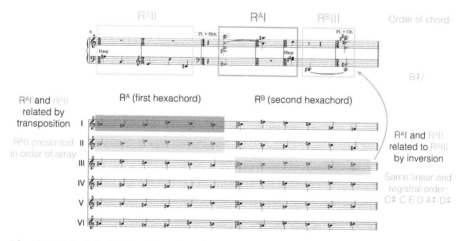

The third block is divided into four fragments. The first three are choral statements, with textural breaks (corresponding to the series hexachords) after each of the three words of the text. There is some instrumental doubling of the choral parts, but these are not shown on the reduced score. The fourth fragment is a sort of instrumental postlude. The first fragment of this block (measure 12) repeats the last fragment of the first block (measure 5). As before, the fragments are linked by common tones, most conspicuously the melodic C♯–D♯ and the chordal E-F-F♯-G sustained in the first fragment and used cadentially at the end of the last fragment.

Divided into four fragments:
three choral statements
and instrumental postlude

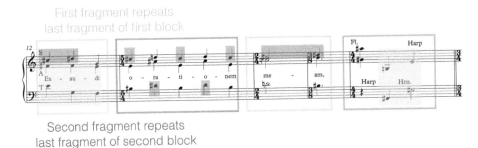

First fragment repeats
last fragment of first block

Second fragment repeats
last fragment of second block

Fragments linked by common tones:
melodic C♯–D♯ and chordal E–F–F♯–G

This block still draws from the rows of the R-array. The first three hexachords, from R^B, are related by transposition. The fourth hexachord, from R^A, is related to these by inversion. Two of the hexachords, R^BI and R^BIII, have been heard before.

The fourth block is a solemn four-voice chorale, with sporadic instrumental doubling (not shown on the reduced score). While the melodic lines, especially the soprano, generally move conjunctly, including many semitones, the spacing of the chords is relatively open, with occasional whole tones but no semitones between adjacent voices. The soprano melody generally moves by the smallest intervals, in combinations of semitones and whole tones. A first upward gesture rises to E. A second gesture rises to D, then pushes beyond to D♯. Those contour highpoints create an additional motivic combination of intervals 1 and 2, with D♯ as the melodic goal.

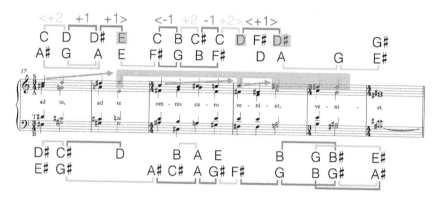

Melodic lines include many whole tones and semitones

Contour highlights E, D, D♯
<-2,+1> motivic combination

Open spacing between voices: no semitones

For this fourth block, Stravinsky abandons the rotational array in favor of a four-part array in which P is paired with I (related by inversion around their shared first note, E♯) and R is paired with IR (related by inversion around their shared first note, A♯). All four forms are presented in retrograde order. In the third chord, Stravinsky incorrectly realized IR's E♯ as G♯. In the final chord, Stravinsky adds G♯ to the array dyad, A♯-E♯. The twelve chords of Stravinsky's chorale correspond to the twelve vertical slices of the four-part array, although Stravinsky's melodic lines do not generally track the pitch-class succession of the rows of the array.

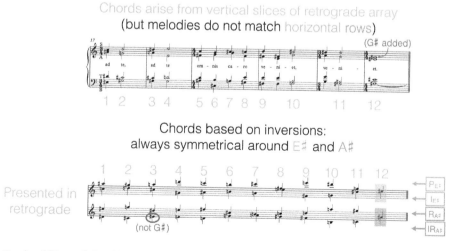

Chords arise from vertical slices of retrograde array
(but melodies do not match horizontal rows)

(G♯ added)

1 2   3 4   5 6 7 8 9   10   11   12

Chords based on inversions:
always symmetrical around E♯ and A♯

1   2   3   4   5   6   7   8   9   10   11   12

Presented in retrograde

(not G♯)

In the fifth and final block, Stravinsky returns to the R^A array, but used now in its vertical rather than horizontal aspect. Vertical 1 is represented by the sustained

A in the contrabass. Verticals 6, 5, 4, 3, and 2, in that order, are heard in the other strings above.

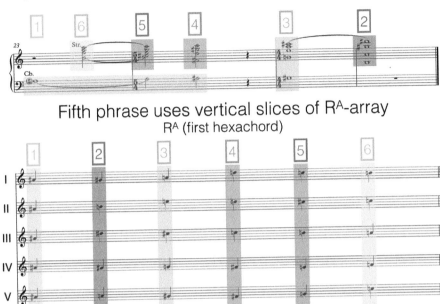

Fifth phrase uses vertical slices of R^A-array
R^A (first hexachord)

Inversional symmetry is inherent in the array. Chord 6 is related to Chord 2 by inversion around A♯ as are Chords 5 and 3. Chord 4 is self-inversional around A♯ as is (trivially) Chord 1. This sense of symmetrical balance around A♯, however, is generally muted in Stravinsky's registral arrangement of the chords.

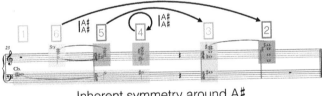

Inherent symmetry around A♯
muted by registral arrangement

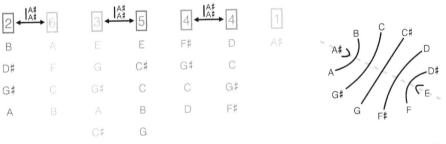

The upper voice moves C–C♯–D♯. As a combination of intervals 1 and 2, it recalls many previous melodic combinations of these intervals and the interest in sc(013) evident beginning in the first block. The final two notes, C♯–D♯, recall many earlier statements of that combination of notes. The cadential arrival on a high D♯ represents the culmination of a great deal of motivic and transformational activity throughout the movement. This music creates meaning in a number of different ways. The slow tempo, widely spaced and slowly moving chords, and preference for chorale texture create an affiliation with solemn, devotional music by Stravinsky and other composers in a long tradition of liturgical music. The motives, melodies, and harmonies create a sense of yearning upward toward D♯, a yearning that is beautifully fulfilled in the final chord of the movement, as a penitent's prayer ascends, and death brings all flesh into the presence of God.

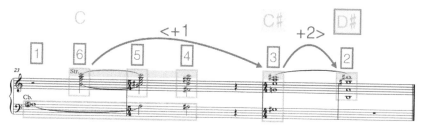

Upper voice: C–C♯–D♯

Interval combination <+1,+2> recalls earlier motives

Final notes C♯–D♯ are common motive
as is cadential arrival on D♯

Ursula Mamlok, *Panta Rhei* for piano, violin, and cello, third movement (1981)

The title, *Panta Rhei*, is a Greek expression that means "everything changes," and this piece is concerned with the gradual transformation of musical objects, especially harmonies. It is scored for three instruments: violin, cello, and piano. There are also three different types of musical material that move among the instruments: a lyrical melody, and two different ostinati on repeated single tones. At the beginning of the movement, the lyrical melody is in the cello. At measure 8, the melody moves to the violin. At the beginning of the movement, the violin is playing an ostinato, a repeated and sustained F♯, punctuated by snap pizzicatos (that's the meaning of the little plus signs in the score); at measure 8, that ostinato, now on D♯, moves to the right hand of the piano. At the beginning of the movement, there is another, different ostinato in the right hand of the piano: short, repeated Ds, with the performance instruction to stop the string inside the piano with a finger of the left hand. At measure 8, that ostinato moves to the cello.

This is a twelve-tone piece, so we begin by looking closely at the twelve-tone series on which it is based. Within each half of the series, that is, within each of its hexachords, the intervals are arranged as an alternation of two intervals: first, 7-9-7-9-7 and then 11-9-11-9-11. Using traditional interval names, the minor third is

The Art of Post-Tonal Analysis. Joseph N. Straus, Oxford University Press. © Joseph N. Straus 2022.
DOI: 10.1093/oso/9780197543979.003.0020

an important interval throughout, combined either with a perfect fifth (in the first hexachord) or a major seventh (in the second hexachord).

Hexachords alternate two intervals

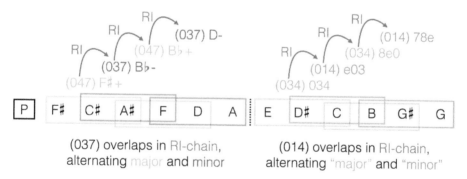

Minor third (9) important in both hexachords
with perfect fifth (7) in first hexachord
or major seventh (11) in second hexachord

Let's see what three-note groupings arise from these pairs of intervals. Within the first hexachord we find four overlapped statements of the consonant triad, (037). The triads alternate major and minor, with the last two notes of one triad becoming the first two notes of the next. Together, the four triads form an RI-chain, leading from F♯ major, through B♭ minor, and B♭ major, to D minor. Within the second hexachord, exactly the same thing happens, only now we're talking about a different type of trichord, namely (014). We overlap what we might call a major form of that trichord, (034), with the bigger interval on the bottom, with what we might call a minor form of the trichord, (014), with the smaller interval at the bottom. If the first half of the series is an RI-chain on (037), the second half is an RI-chain on (014).

(037) overlaps in RI-chain,
alternating major and minor

(014) overlaps in RI-chain,
alternating "major" and "minor"

The two hexachords of the series are both hexatonic hexachords. The hexatonic collection can be thought of as a scale of alternating 1 and 3. The hexatonic hexachord can also be thought of as two augmented triads a semitone apart, and the series features the augmented triads as every other note.

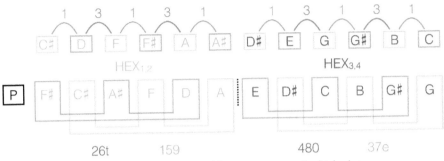

Each hexachord is two augmented triads
every other note of the series

This passage uses just two forms of the series: P from the beginning through measure 7 and I from measure 7 to measure 15. In the presentation of both forms, two notes are plucked out to serve as the ostinato pitches: F♯ and D from P and D♯ and G in the same order positions in I. The lyrical melody advances slowly through the series, with constant recall and repeat of earlier notes.

The two series forms, P and I, have the same hexachords but in reverse order. If we think of each of the two hexachords as defining a harmonic area, the large-scale motion of the passage establishes one area, moves through another, then returns to its starting point: first oriented toward $HEX_{1,2}$; then oriented toward $HEX_{3,4}$, including the last six notes of P and the first 6 notes of I; and finally a return to the opening $HEX_{1,2}$.

We can also parse the piece into a progression of trichords. First, we get four consonant triads, alternating major and minor, then four (014)s, alternating the major and minor forms of that trichord. When the I-form of the series starts in measure 9, we get the same thing again: four consonant triads, and then four (014)s.

In Phrase 1A, the first six notes of P, we get four triads, alternating major and minor. In the progression from triad to triad, one note moves by semitone while the other two hold. In each case, we can imagine the move as an inversional flip: the two held notes form an axis around which the moving note flips symmetrically. Compare that to what happens in Phrase 2A, involving the first six notes of I. There we again get four triads, and again we alternate major and minor, and again two notes hold while one note moves by semitone. The voice leading among these triads is as

smooth as it can be. In each case, we can imagine the move as an inversional flip: the
two held notes form an axis around which the moving note flips symmetrically.

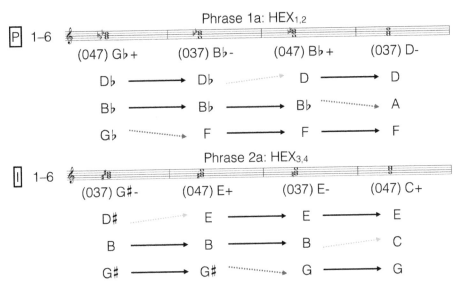

Something rather similar happens in the progression among trichords in (014) in
Phrases 1B and 2B. Again, two notes hold while the moving voice flips symmetrically around them. The voice leading is not so smooth however—the moving voice
always moves by 5 semitones. But because of the common tones, there is still a
strong sense of connectedness among the chords in the progression.

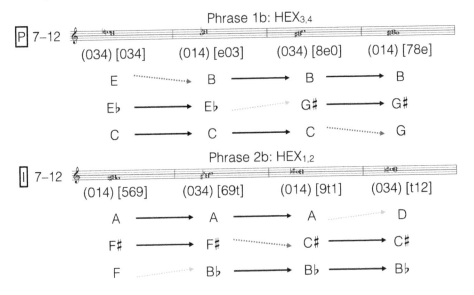

It can be revealing to trace these progressions on a hexatonic cycle. The outer
circles on these cycles arrange the six notes of a hexatonic collection into six triads,
connected in the ways we have just discussed: two notes hold and one note moves
by semitone each time. The inner circles on these cycles arrange the same six notes

of a hexatonic collection as six (014)s, connected by having two notes hold and the remaining note flip around them. The music can be understood to trace systematic paths on these cycles.

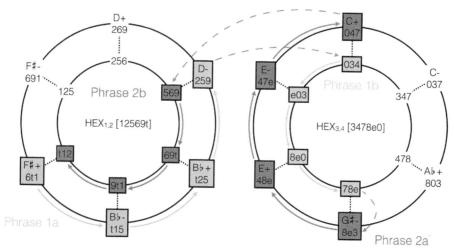

There is a systematic aspect to the rhythm, too, at least as far as the two ostinato lines are concerned. Ostinato 1 projects a regular periodicity of 17 sixteenth notes: 10.5 sixteenth notes for the sounding duration of the F♯, cut off by the snap pizz, and then a rest of 6.5 sixteenth notes. Ostinato 2 has a regular periodicity of eleven sixteenth notes: that is the duration between the attacked Ds. The periodicities of the two ostinatos do not coincide with each other, and neither coincides in any simple way with the beats of the notated $\frac{3}{4}$ meter. There may also be a systematic aspect to the rhythms of the lyrical melody, but that is less certain. It might be better to imagine that the piece is built on a contrast between the relatively rigid ostinatos and the relatively free melody. The result is a kaleidoscopic rhythmic interplay.

Rhythmic regularity in ostinatos contrasts relatively free melody

Ostinato 1: 17 sixteenths periodicity = 10.5 sixteenth notes + 6.5 sixteenth rests

Ostinato 2: 11 sixteenths periodicity

21

Elliott Carter, *Riconoscenza per Goffredo Petrassi* for solo violin (1984)

This passage presents three contrasting types of material, distinguished in obvious ways: the A material is flowing and legato with wide leaps, marked *dolce legatissimo scorrevole*; the B material is focused into small chromatic clusters amid violent bursts of activity (marked *giocosamenta furioso martellato*); the C material (*tranquillo, ben legato*) consists of slowly changing, sustained dyads. The materials are presented mostly one at a time (first A, then B, then A again, then C), but there are two brief intrusions of B into A, and C begins before the second statement of A has finished. The music is designed as a portrait in sound of the Italian composer Goffredo Petrassi, who evidently had a somewhat mercurial personality, by turns energetically active, brusque, and quietly contemplative.

The A material is mainly concerned with the intervals 3 and 6. Every note is connected by either 3 or 6 to the note before and/or after it.

The Art of Post-Tonal Analysis. Joseph N. Straus, Oxford University Press. © Joseph N. Straus 2022.
DOI: 10.1093/oso/9780197543979.003.0021

As a result, there are lots of diminished seventh chords (0369), sometimes represented by a constituent diminished triad (036) or by just a dyad (03) or (06).

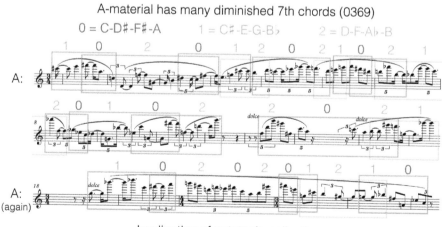

In the combinations of these diminished seventh chords, there is always the implication, and in some cases the reality, of octatonic collections.

A-material has many diminished 7th chords (0369)

0 = C-D♯-F♯-A   1 = C♯-E-G-B♭   2 = D-F-A♭-B

Implication of octatonic collections:

$OCT_{0,1}$ $OCT_{1,2}$ $OCT_{0,2}$

In a similar way, the B section is also concerned with two intervals: 1 and 2. Every note is connected to the note before and/or after it by one of those intervals, and the larger groupings are often chromatic trichords (012) or tetrachords (0123), within a largely chromatic world.

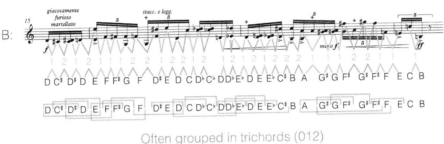

B-material primarily uses intervals 1 and 2

Often grouped in trichords (012)
and/or tetrachords (0123)

The C section is preoccupied with the two remaining interval classes: 4 and 5. It presents these intervals as slow, sustained dyads (to complete the pattern, I have inserted an implied G above the sustained D; this implied note is provided in the music by a prominent G in the ongoing A-section material). Combinations of 4 and 5 into tetrachords produce forms of (0146). This is one of the two "all-interval tetrachords," so called because they contain one instance of each of the six different interval classes. The other all-interval tetrachord is (0137), and we will be making its acquaintance shortly. The (0146) in this passage are related by inversion around the two notes shared by adjacent form: the first and third chords are related by inversion around the shared E-G♯; the second and fourth chords are related by inversion around the shared F-B♭. All three forms of (0146) belong to the same octatonic collection (OCT$_{1,2}$).

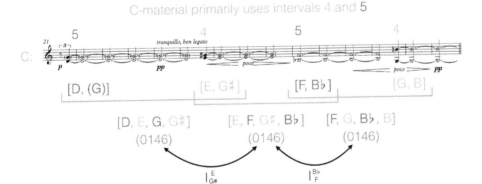

C-material primarily uses intervals 4 and 5

The three (0146) = OCT$_{1,2}$

So far we have imagined the A, B, and C materials as almost completely distinct from each other both in mood and intervallic focus.

Material	Intervals	Trichords	Tetrachords	Collections
A material	(6) (05)	(024)	(0358)	Octatonic
B material	(01) (02)	(012)	(0123)	Chromatic
C material	(04) (05)		(0146)	Octatonic

But there are also subtle links among them. Let's consider first the links between the B and C material. In the C material, while the vertical dyads (4 and 5) and tetrachords (0146) are distinctive to the C material, the melodic intervals that connect the vertical dyads are all 1 and 2 (the melodic intervals of the B material).

C-material has B-material melodic intervals of 1 and 2

Conversely, the C material's (0146), and its intervallic partner (0137), the other all-interval tetrachord, play a role in B. Two forms of (0146) are outlined among (mostly) the highest notes of B, while a form of (0137), the other all-interval tetrachord, is formed by the lowest notes.

B-material features C-material's (0146) in highest notes

The A material has extensive links with both B and C, links that involve the two all-interval tetrachords, (0146) and (0137). Within the A material, we had been concerned with (03) and (06), and had grouped them together when they belonged to the *same* diminished seventh chord.

A different perspective on the A material opens up when we consider that (03) and (06) belong to *different* diminished seventh chord. Tritones abound in the A material, formed either by adjacent notes, or separated by a single note. Every combination of a tritone with a minor third from a different diminished seventh chord produces a form of either (0146) or (0137). In this passage, there are nineteen all-interval tetrachords, all formed by combining a tritone and a minor third from different diminished seventh chords. These two all-interval tetrachords are the essential building blocks for much of Carter's music.

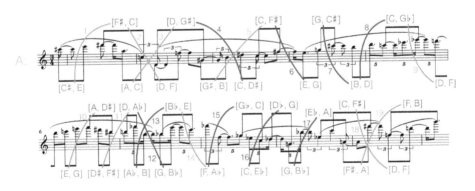

These nineteen 0146 and 0137, produced by combinations of (03) and (06) belonging to different (0369), can be traced on an appropriate musical space. The nodes of the space are the six tritones and the twelve minor thirds. The connecting lines join them to produce one of the all-interval tetrachords. In general, the music begins by creating all-interval tetrachords that refer to the tritone C-F♯, then move away and back toward it.

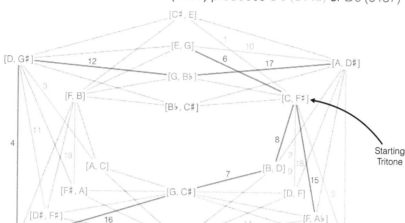

Within A: Tritone + m3 from different (0369) produces C's (0146) or B's (0137)

The all-interval tetrachords in the B and C sections, although not partitioned into (03) + (06), can also be located in this space. All of the all-interval tetrachords in the B and C sections have already been prefigured in the A section. The contrasting sections are thus linked in subtle ways. And that brings us back to the mercurial Signor Petrassi. His personality has obvious contrasts and seeming incongruities, but to a sympathetic friend (like Elliott Carter), the disparate parts are understood to harmonize together within an attractive whole.

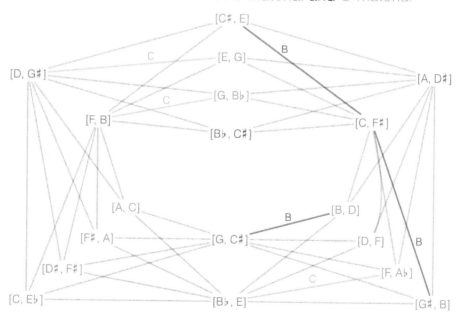

All-interval tetrachords in B-material and C-material

22

Tania León, *Rituál* (1987)

This passage, which comes right after a long, slow, pensive introduction, is the first section of a fleet, light-footed, dazzling dance, a sort of scherzo, that works its way up from the lowest note of the piano keyboard to the registral heights.

Amid the increasingly rapid rhythmic activity and the short stabs of color, there are only seven different pitch events in the passage. These are presented mostly in this order, and thus in generally ascending motion from the lowest note on the piano keyboard to D5-E♭5. The C (event 2) is sometimes heard an octave lower. Other than that, these events are fixed in pitch.

The Art of Post-Tonal Analysis. Joseph N. Straus, Oxford University Press. © Joseph N. Straus 2022.
DOI: 10.1093/oso/9780197543979.003.0022

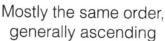

Mostly the same order,
generally ascending

The pitches are arranged to give a sense of directed motion from the initial low A to the terminal D-E♭. The second note, C, lies 27 semitones above A. The final E♭ lies 27 semitones above that C, which thus bisects the total pitch space.

Similarly, starting on the C♯ in the middle of the trichord in event 3, we can imagine a chain of 7s that carry us up to the same E♭—the second stage of that journey, from G♯ to E♭, is also divided symmetrically.

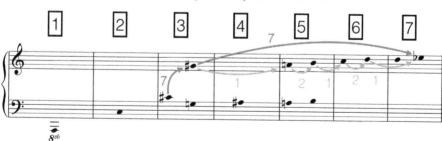

A chain of alternating 7 and 6 similarly directs the motion, in this case toward the high D within the final dyad. The upper stage of this journey, too, is divided symmetrically.

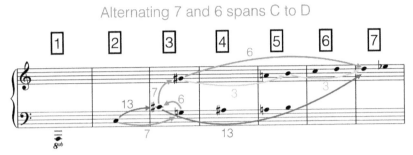

C♯ divides total space into 13+13   G♯ to D divided symmetrically

The final stage of the upward journey is evidently octatonic, deploying a scale of alternating 1 and 2.

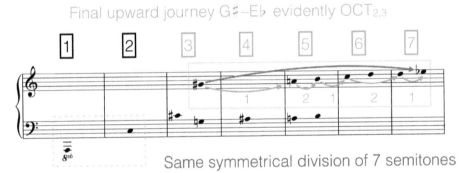

A and C: OCT$_{2,3}$ Same symmetrical division of 7 semitones

But the sense of hexatonic affiliation is even more pronounced, as chains of alternating 1 and 3 permeate the progression and, together with the symmetrical moves, direct the motion upward from the first note to the last.

Hexatonic: chains of 1 and 3 throughout

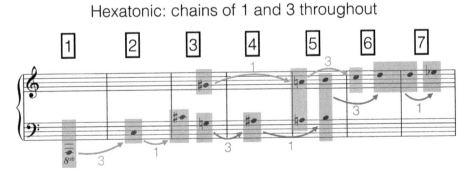

HEX$_{0,1}$ to start   Nearly complete HEX$_{2,3}$ overlaps

The music navigates through space in four phases. In the first phase, we find six brief variations. After the first, abrupt one-measure introduction, the variations all

last for two measures and include the first five of the seven pitch events. The order of
the events is strictly maintained. Low A and low C act as metrical timekeepers and
all of the events mostly maintain a fixed position within the measure. The variations
differ only slightly, and with the fixity of the pitches, invite us to attend closely to
subtle changes in the rhythm.

Phase 1: variations are two measures, first five pitch events used in strict order

Lowest A and low C are metrical timekeepers, all events mostly in fixed metrical position

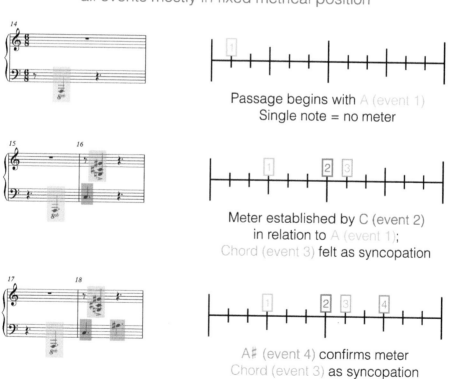

Passage begins with A (event 1)
Single note = no meter

Meter established by C (event 2)
in relation to A (event 1);
Chord (event 3) felt as syncopation

A♯ (event 4) confirms meter
Chord (event 3) as syncopation

A (event 1) and C (event 2) stable in place,
chord (event 3) and A♯ (event 4) compressed
to make room for A-B (event 5) heard twice

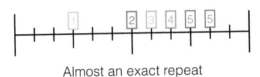

Almost an exact repeat

Second measure almost the same
First time C (event 2) is octave lower
Low A (event 1) is early offbeat,
foreshadowing rhythmic play

In the second phase, actions that took two measures in the first phase are now compressed into a single measure. In this phase, there are eight variations, still using only the first five of the seven pitch events. As before, events may shift around a bit within the variation, but the ordering of the events remains strict. Although events occur in the prescribed order, an event may be omitted within a variation. For example, C (the second event) sometimes substitutes for A (the first event) as the timekeeper on the downbeat. All of the variations end the same way, with events 3, 4, and 5. Through this entire second phase, the relative position of the events (the order in which they occur) stays the same, but their location within the measure may change. At the beginning of the phase, the movement of events from location to location is not well coordinated, but by the end of the phase, we become aware of a regular alternation, as the events shift forward and back in relation to the underlying meter.

Phase 2: variations now single measure
Still using 5 pitch events
Strict order but some might be omitted

All variations end with
events 3, 4, and 5

Metric position can change:
uncoordinated at first,
then regularly shift forward and back

Low A (event 1) returns to downbeat
Chord (event 3) skips over C (event 2)
A♯ (event 4) returns to downbeat
A-B (event 5) jumps up not down

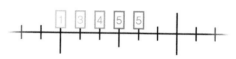

A♯ (event 4) shifts earlier to offbeat
So does A-B (event 5), now on the beat
Variation compressed to 5 eighth notes

C (event 2) replaces low A (event 1)
A♯ (event 4) and single A-B (event 5) shift later

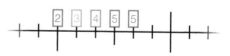

C (event 2) remains on downbeat
Chord (event 3) remains of offbeat
A♯ (event 4) and A-B (event 5) compressed

Low A (event 1) subs back in, but enters early
Chord (event 3) now takes downbeat role
A♯ (event 4) and first A-B (event 5) follow
Second A-B stretches variation to 7 eighth notes

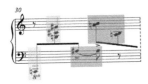

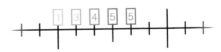

Variation compresses to 5 eighth notes again
Low A (event 1) and chord (event 3) back in place
followed by A♯ (event 4) and A-B (event 5)

Early-arriving C (event 2) replaces low A (event 1)
Downbeat chord (event 3), A♯ (event 4) follows
A-B (event 5) single attack

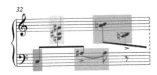

C (event 2) remains, now on downbeat
Chord (event 3) and A♯ (event 4) follow
A-B (event 5) downbeat and octave leap
Variation again compressed to 5 beats

In the third phase, the sixth and penultimate pitch event is introduced: the whole-tone dyad C-D. The order of the events is now sometimes scrambled, although A and C retain their timekeeper role at the beginning of each variation. At the end of the phase, three events are pared away (we lose C, A-B, and the recently introduced C-D). The result is a process of compression that forms a transition to the next and final phrase.

Phase 3: order
sometimes scrambled

Low A (event 1) and C (event 2)
remain opening timekeepers

C-D (event 6) is introduced

Three events disappear during phase:
C (event 2), A-B (event 5), C-D (event 6)

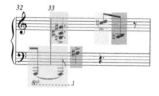

Low A (event 1) returns, but early offbeat
Chord (event 3) becomes timekeeper
Sneak preview of C-D (event 6)
A-B (event 5) is first scrambled entrance

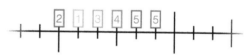

C (event 2) becomes the downbeat
Low A (event 1) overcompensates,
now both late and out of order
A-B (event 5) regains octave leap

C (event 2) and A♯ (event 4) on downbeats
Chord (event 3) and A-B (event 5) away from A♯

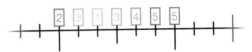

C (event 2) is downbeat timekeeper
Low A (event 1) pushed further right
Chord (event 3) is repeated
Variation extended to 7 beats

Shortest, sparsest variation yet
C (event 2) pushed off downbeat
Chord (event 3) remains on the beat
A♯ (event 4) immediately follows

Events 1, 2, 3, and 4 in order: feels like a restoration
C–D (event 6) as replacement of A-B (event 5)
Final statement of C (event 2), begins liquidation

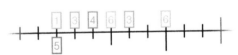

Events 1, 3, 4, and 6 underlying order maintained
Final statement of A-B (event 5) joins downbeat
Chord (event 3) and C-D (event 6) are repeated
Variation extended to seven beats

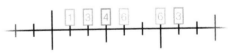

Same core of events 1, 3, 4, and 6 in normal order
Low A (event 1) pushed off the downbeat
Two-event tag: C-D (event 6) and chord (event 3)

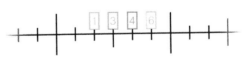

Variation compressed to only four beats
Same core of events 1, 3, 4, and 6 in order
Final statement of C-D (event 6)

Phase 4: explosion into wild dance
Regularity of order and meter shattered
Only events 1, 3, 4, and 7 remain

Low A (event 1)
initiates all variations

D-E♭ (event 7) sets off
a musical celebration

D-E♭ generally leaps to/from low A
Recapitulates passage's journey from A to D-E♭

In the fourth and final phase, the music explodes into a wild dance. The regularities of order and meter that had previously been challenged are now shattered. We find groups of variable size and density, all initiated by the low A. After the compression and streamlining at the end of the previous phase, only four events are now in play: the low A, the three-note chord, A♯, and finally the climactic high D-E♭. This dyad is the culmination of a number of intervallic processes, and its arrival sets of a musical celebration, with its iterations resounding like the pealing of a bell. It generally occurs as the last event in a variation followed by a vast leap down to the low A at the beginning of the next variation, and thus recapitulating (in reverse order) the journey of the passage as a whole.

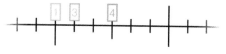

Events 1 (A), 3 (chord), and 4 (A♯) in order
Still $\frac{6}{8}$ meter, but that will disappear soon

Climactic D-E♭ (event 7) on a downbeat
Events 1, 3, 4, and 7 in order
Extra chord (event 3) at the end
Clear sense of $\frac{6}{8}$ meter

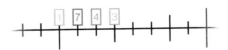

Low A (event 1) still initiation point
A♯ (event 4) same offbeat position
Chord (event 3) and D-E♭ (event 7) swap places
Variation is 4 beats, $\frac{6}{8}$ meter is weakened

Same with extra D-E♭ (event 7) at the end
Low A (event 1) entrance middle of $\frac{8}{8}$ measure
$\frac{6}{8}$ meter fatally undermined

Low A (event 1) and A♯ (event 4) stay in place
Chord (event 3) and D-E♭ (event 7) switch back
Extra chord (event 3) at the end

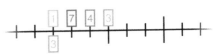

Chord (event 3) and D-E♭ (event 7) switch again
Low A (event 1) and A♯ (event 4) stay again
Extra chord (event 3) on top of low A (event 1)

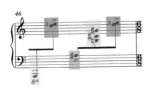

5-beat variation, same order of events: 1, 7, 4, 3
Extra D-E♭ (event 7) at the end
Repetition highlights metric displacement

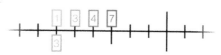

Another four-beat variation
Chord (event 3) and D-E♭ (event 7) switch again
Extra chord (event 3) on top of low A (event 1)

Order maintained from previous variation
Expanded by repetition of A♯ (event 4)

Compressed to only three beats
D-E♭ (event 7) omitted for the first time

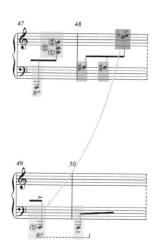

Expansion back to five beats:
Repetition of low A (event 1)
Reinstatement of D-E♭ (event 7)
Last variation with all four events

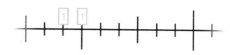

Low A (event 1) heard twice
Return to first measure, return to 6/8 meter
Last interval: D-E♭ (event 7) to low A (event 1)
Recaps (in reverse) journey of whole passage

23

Tan Dun, *Intercourse of Fire and Water* for solo cello (1996)

This piece begins with a musical block that plays a constructive role throughout the piece, occurring in its entirety either at its original level or transposed. This block divides into three smaller phrases (we'll call them A, B, and C) separated by long silences. A, B, and C are highly contrasting, in ways that are suggestive of the title of the work: the A material is slow and introspective—a smooth wave up and back down; the B material is fiery and furious, loud and agitated; the C material intensifies the fiery qualities of the B material.

Musical block X: occurs in its entirety throughout piece, at pitch or transposed
Divided into three phrases (A, B, and C) separated by long silences

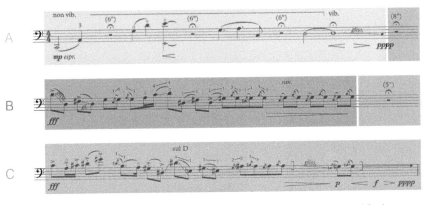

A is a smooth wave   B and C are fiery and furious

The Art of Post-Tonal Analysis. Joseph N. Straus, Oxford University Press. © Joseph N. Straus 2022.
DOI: 10.1093/oso/9780197543979.003.0023

The A material is a series of nine pitches, representing the five notes of a pentatonic collection: C-D-E-G-A (all of the notes except E are heard twice). The last six pitches of the melody are arranged as an RI-chain, alternating <+2, –9> with <–9, +2>.

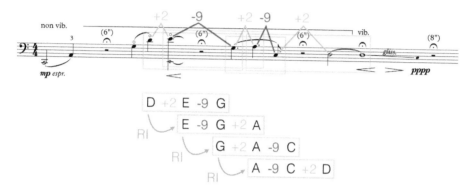

All four links in the chain represent (025). And there are two more members of the same trichord type overlapped in the first five notes, although with different adjacent intervals. [G, A, C] and [D, E, G] occur both before and within the RI-chain.

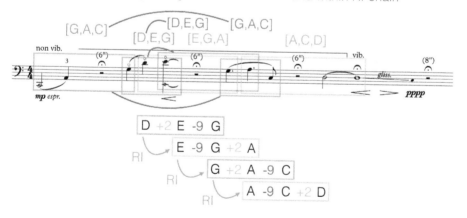

This pentatonic collection is inversionally symmetrical on the axis D-G♯. The last six notes are arranged symmetrically in pitch around an unsounded G♯3.

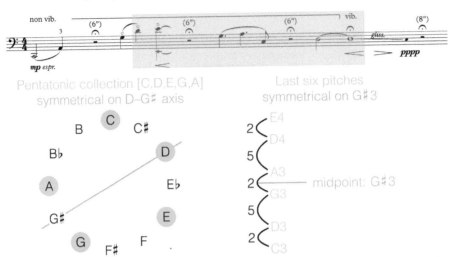

That unsounded G♯3 in the A material sounds prominently in the B material that follows. The B material thus makes explicit something that was merely implied in A. And within the B material, the G♯ lies halfway between the octave Ds at the beginning, and is locally embellished by grace notes B (3 semitones above) and E♯ (3 semitones below).

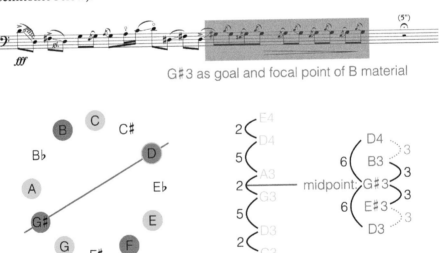

The B material contrasts in many obvious ways with the A material: it is fast, brusque, and very loud while the A material was slow, lyrical, and very soft. But there are points of connection also that extend beyond their mutual interest in inversional symmetry around G♯. In the first half of the B melody, we find a repeat of the last six notes of the A melody. The intervals are different, alternating <+2, +3>

with <+3, +2>, but they still form an RI-chain involving (025) with four links, and the still lie within the same pentatonic collection.

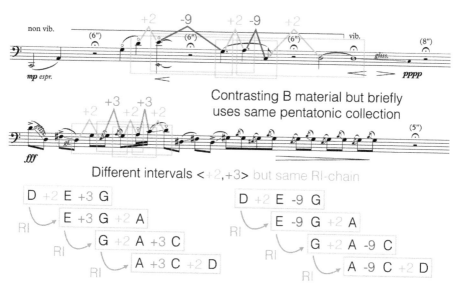

Two additional forms of (025) are heard in the second half of the B material, and they, too, are arranged as an RI-chain. This RI-chain adds four new notes (D♯, F♯, G♯, and B) and strongly implies a new pentatonic collection, from which only C♯ is absent. For the most part, the pentatonic collection of the A section and the first half of the B section has simply been transposed down a semitone. In these contrasting pentatonic collections, we get the most potent realization of a dramatic dichotomy that underpins the music, juxtaposing mostly white-note collections with mostly sharp-note collections. The A material uses only the white notes. The B material moves from mostly white notes to mostly sharp notes.

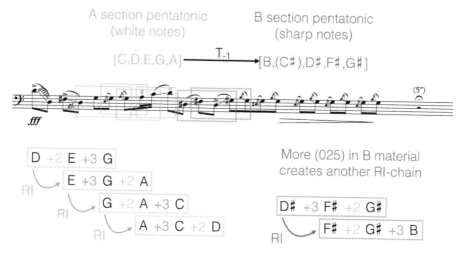

In the C material, white-note and sharp-note materials are somewhat intermingled, while the focus on (025) and chains of (025) remains. The final note of the section (G) returns as the first note of the subsequent section, which transposes the whole block up a perfect fifth (not shown here).

The three sections navigate between two distinct sound worlds, defined by the natural hexachord (G-A-B-C-D-E) and the complementary sharp hexachord (C♯-D♯-E♯-F♯-G♯-A♯). The music can be parsed into ten fragments, five belonging to each of the contrasting hexachords. The first two fragments, comprising the A section, belong to the natural hexachord. The fragments then alternate between the two hexachords until the final two fragments, which belong to the sharp hexachord.

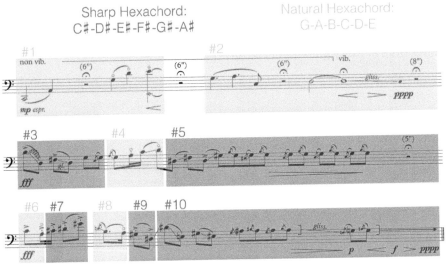

Within each hexachord, the fragments are connected by webs of common tones (solid lines), or tones that deviate by only one or two semitones from the previous fragment (dotted lines). Within each hexachord, the music moves from a pentatonic collection to its T_7.

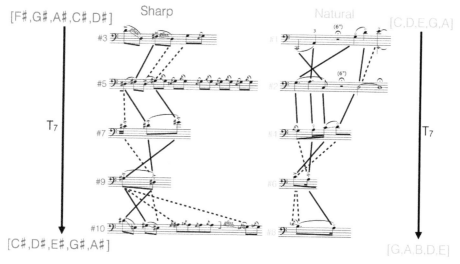

Visualized on the traditional circle of fifths, the entire aggregate of twelve notes is divided into two complementary hexachords, each of which contains two overlapping pentatonic scales. There is a clear programmatic meaning to this fundamental opposition of complementary hexachords, one related to the title of the piece, *Intercourse of Fire and Water*. The A material suggests water—cool, placid, slow in its movements. The B and C material suggest fire—light and fleet in its movements, hot and agitated. But despite their fundamental contrast, there are significant points of contact between the watery and fiery musics, especially their mutual interest in diatonic hexachords, pentatonic scales, and (025) trichords, isolated or gathered into chains. And while the A music is pure water, the B and C musics witness interpenetration of natural and sharp hexachords—a musical evocation of the intercourse of fire and water.

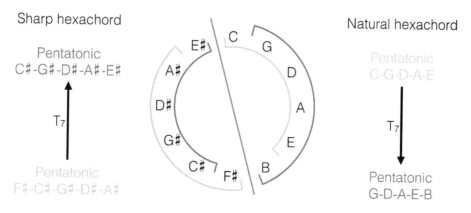

Circle of fifths split into complementary hexachords

Each hexachord contains two overlapping pentatonic scales

24

Shulamit Ran, *Soliloquy* for violin, cello, and piano (1997)

This passage, a brief prelude to a substantial one-movement piece, can be thought of as an elaboration of the A major triad with which it begins and ends.

The Art of Post-Tonal Analysis. Joseph N. Straus, Oxford University Press. © Joseph N. Straus 2022.
DOI: 10.1093/oso/9780197543979.003.0024

Over the course of the passage, notes are added one at a time until the aggregate of all twelve notes is complete.

Each stage of the accretion of notes around the central A major triad provides a different and evolving context for that central harmony.

Stage	New note	Cumulative Total Collection												Comment
		G♯	A	B♭	B	C	C♯	D	D♯	E	F	F♯	G	
1	A		A											A is centric tone
2	E		A							E				A supported by perfect fifth E
3	C♯		A				C♯			E				Triad completed
4	B♭		A	B♭			C♯			E				B♭ is upper neighbor to A
5	F		A	B♭			C♯			E	F			F is upper neighbor to E
6	D		A	B♭			C♯	D		E	F			D is upper neighbor to C♯
7	F♯		A	B♭			C♯	D		E	F	F♯		F♯ completes one semitone cluster. HEX₁,₂ (omitting E)
8	C		A	B♭		C	C♯	D		E	F	F♯		C is lower neighbor to C♯. Second semitone cluster complete.
9	G♯	G♯	A	B♭		C	C♯	D		E	F	F♯		Lower neighbor to A. Third semitone cluster complete. Complete enneatonic collection.
10	D♯	G♯	A	B♭		C	C♯	D	D♯	E	F	F♯		D♯ is lower neighbor to E. Fills in gap. Initiates complementary augmented triad D♯–G–B.
11	G	G♯	A	B♭		C	C♯	D	D♯	E	F	F♯	G	Fills in gap. Continues complementary triad.
12	B	G♯	A	B♭	B	C	C♯	D	D♯	E	F	F♯	G	Fills in final gap. Aggregate complete.

Treating the series of new notes as a basic structure for the passage, we can see the extent to which the piece is conceived as a succession of major, minor, and augmented triads.

Succession of major, minor, and augmented triads

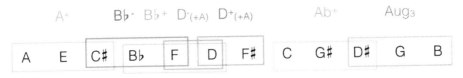

The complexities of the musical surface often present these triads partially or weakly, but at the same time suggest additional triads (notably an A minor triad near the end).

These triads relate to each other in familiar ways (via L, P, and SLIDE) and can thus be traced on the space known as Cube Dances: a long voyage away from home and back again. Large harmonic regions are defined by two of the four hexatonic collections and the enneatonic collection that subsumes them. (An enneatonic collection consists of any three augmented triads, or any two hexatonic collections that share an augmented triad).

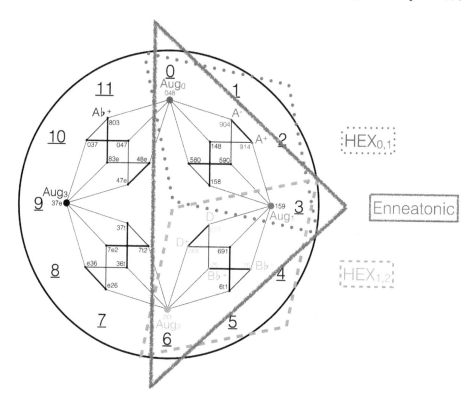

Within that larger harmonic environment, the triads progress from a starting point on A major, via SLIDE to a different hexatonic collection, within that hexatonic via P and L, via T_6 to yet another hexatonic collection (lying outside the prevailing enneatonic), and then back to A minor (via SLIDE) and A major (via P).

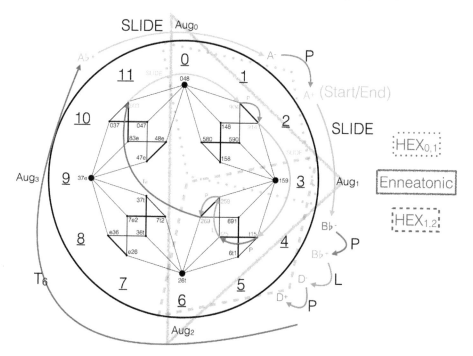

Here is that triadic progression traced on the score.

While the triadic progression is a primary harmonic layer, the triadic unfolding leaves other sets in its wake, including especially forms of (014).

And like the triads, these (014) can be mapped on a modified Cube Dances, where hexatonic cycles of (014) are created from chains of L (invert around the semitone) and R (invert around the minor third).

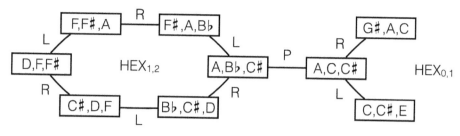

We start on a (014) that combines A-C♯ (from the A major triad) with a dissonant B♭. We then progress in a purposeful hexatonic way to [FF♯A]. At that point we leap (via R-SLIDE) to a different hexatonic collection, and then end on [ACC♯]. The first (014) combined A-C♯ with B♭. The concluding (014) combines A-C♯ with C. After a long journey, we find ourselves back roughly where we began.

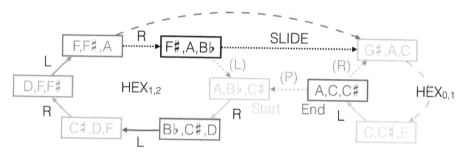

Here is the progression of (014) traced on the score.

25

Kaija Saariaho, *Papillons* for solo cello, No. 3 (2000)

This short movement for solo cello gives the impression of a single, fixed harmony animated in diverse ways and made to shimmer with colors. It has a somewhat ghostly quality—the ethereal high register, the tremolos, the *sul ponticello* playing, the string harmonics. It is to be played *calmo, con tristezza* (calmly and with sadness), and sounds in many ways like the lament of someone almost prostrate with grief, expressed through long descending lines, featuring the descending semitone, that traditional musical sorrowful sigh. The movement as a whole uses only seven different notes: the six notes of $HEX_{1,2}$ (D-F-F♯-A-B♭-C♯) plus the note G, heard only fleetingly in two places. The music strongly emphasizes D as a generative bass tone, establishing it as scale-degree $\hat{1}$ for a hexatonic scale.

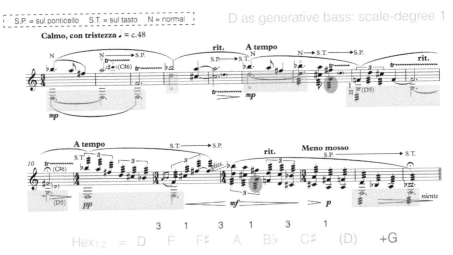

The notes tend to occur in a particular order, and one might imagine that a seven-note series is operating in the piece, often unfolding over a drone on D. The series mostly follows the descending scalar order, starting on B♭, tacking the anomalous G onto the end.

The Art of Post-Tonal Analysis. Joseph N. Straus, Oxford University Press. © Joseph N. Straus 2022.
DOI: 10.1093/oso/9780197543979.003.0025

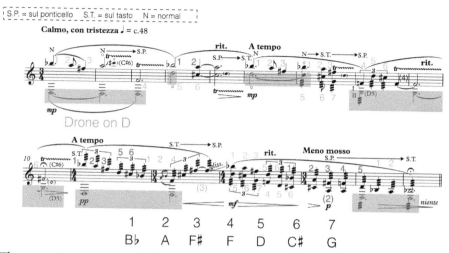

	1	2	3	4	5	6	7
	B♭	A	F♯	F	D	C♯	G

The recurring segments of the series act as motives in the piece. B♭-A-F♯ is particularly prominent, as is D-C♯. Those descending semitones, especially the B♭-A, are traditional musical emblems of grief.

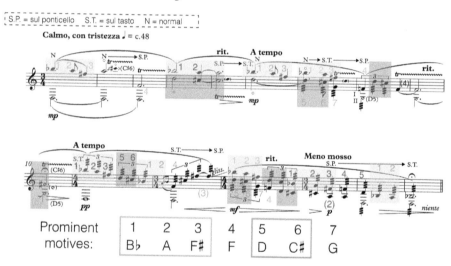

Prominent motives:	1	2	3	4	5	6	7
	B♭	A	F♯	F	D	C♯	G

Just as the repertoire of pitch classes is severely restricted (with only seven different pitch classes in use), the inventory of pitches is similarly narrow, with only sixteen different pitches. Two of the pitch classes (the hexatonic F and the non-hexatonic G) are heard in only one register, as F4 and G4. The rest are heard in two or three different registers. For the most part, the pitches are arranged in scalar or near scalar order, with repetitions of the familiar hexatonic alternation of 1 and 3. But D3 is separated from its nearest registral neighbor by a full seven semitones, and this resonant perfect fifth adds to the sense of D as a root and generator of the harmonies heard above it.

PC	D	F	F♯	A	B♭	C♯	(G)
# of registers	3	1	2	3	3	3	1

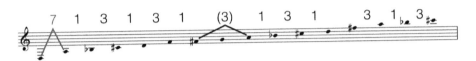

The hexatonic collection is rich in triadic subsets. HEX$_{1,2}$ contains major and minor triads on D, F♯, and B♭.

Triadic subsets of Hex$_{1,2}$

Dm   DM   F♯m   F♯M   B♭m   B♭M

Although none of these triads is ever heard in its entirety directly in the music, they nonetheless haunt the music. That is particularly true of D major/minor. Because of the persistence of D in the lower registers, and because of its support by the A immediately above it (without intervening pitches), it takes on a centric role, and it draws F/F♯ and A into its orbit. The same is true to a lesser extent of F♯ and B♭—there are hints of B♭ major/minor and F♯ major/minor throughout the movement. Take the final two measures as an example: Does the piece end in D (major or minor), but with B♭ substituting for A? Or does it end in B♭ major (in first inversion), with the A acting as leading tone to B♭? The tonal ambiguity is of a piece with the shimmering, evocative musical surface of the entire piece.

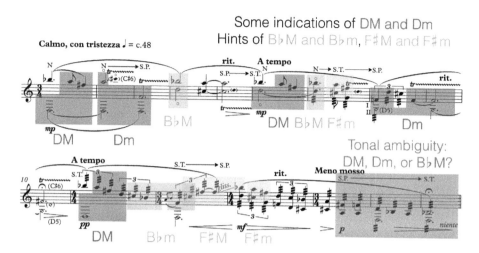

26

Joan Tower, *Vast Antique Cubes* (2000)

This passage has a somewhat dreamy quality: it's very soft, with scalar wisps of sound rising up into the ether. It features two extended ascending scales. The first is $OCT_{1,2}$, ascending through more than an octave in alternating semitones and whole tones. The second is WT_1, ascending in parallel 4s through more than two octaves.

Taking these scales as a point of entry, we can parse the entire passage into whole-tone and octatonic collections, with some areas of overlap or ambiguity. The collections articulate the form of the passage: after a dyadic introduction, we have a mostly octatonic middle, and a mostly whole-tone ending.

The Art of Post-Tonal Analysis. Joseph N. Straus, Oxford University Press. © Joseph N. Straus 2022.
DOI: 10.1093/oso/9780197543979.003.0026

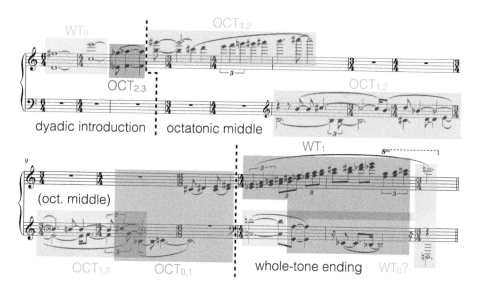

The piece explores subtle links and affinities among the contrasting collections. Compare the two dyads in mm. 1–2 with the two dyads in m. 3. In the first pair, two 4s are related by T_{-2}, resulting in a whole-tone formation (0246). In the second pair, two 3s are related by T_{+2}, resulting in an octatonic formation (0235). Or one can focus on the 2s as the primary units, connected by either T_4 or T_3. With that in mind, we might think of the lowest four notes in the passage as involving another pair of 2s related by transposition.

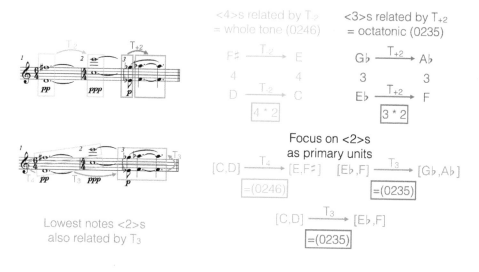

The 2s are common elements between whole-tone and octatonic collections: when they are combined by T_4, the result is a whole-tone formation; when they are combined at T_3, the result is an octatonic formation. Furthermore, any individual 2 might belong to either a whole-tone or an octatonic collection, and might act as a pivot between them.

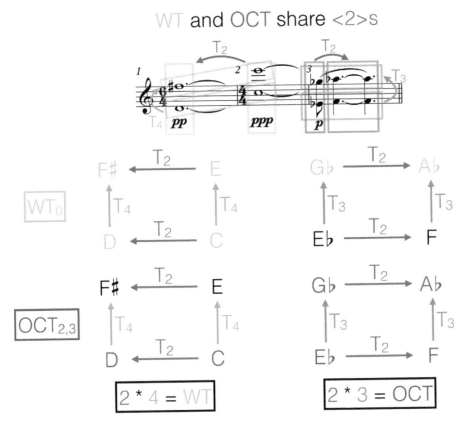

The ascending octatonic scale that follows ($OCT_{1,2}$) can also be parsed as combinations of 2s, starting and ending as it does with B-C♯. So can the imitative passage that follows, still within $OCT_{1,2}$, and still emphasizing B-C♯.

The octatonic and whole-tone fragments that lead to the conclusion of the passage can be similarly parsed into whole-tones.

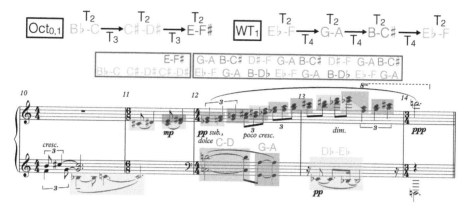

OCT and WT fragments organized as combinations of <2>s

Within an octatonic or a whole-tone collection, the 2s combine in consistent ways to produce tetrachords and the entire larger collection. And the intersections among the collections provide audible sources of continuity among them.

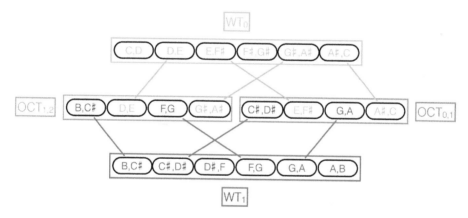

One can envision the passage as moving through a space that consists of 2s connected either by T_3 (forming octatonic collections) or by T_4 (forming whole-tone collections). The space is a torus, wrapping around on itself both horizontally and vertically.

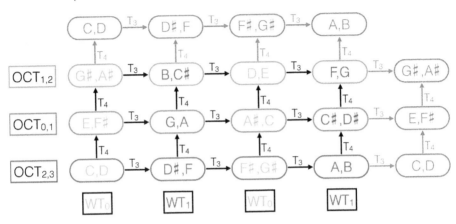

The piece begins with two pairs of dyads, one moving vertically through the space (WT_0) and the other moving horizontally ($OCT_{2,3}$). The dyad C-D is shared between the collections, and the lowest six notes of the passage all belong to $OCT_{2,3}$.

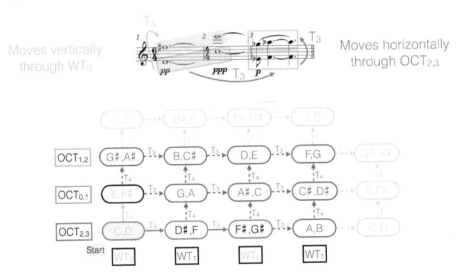

The ascending scale and the imitative passage that follow are confined to the four whole-tones of $OCT_{1,2}$, with particular emphasis on B-C♯.

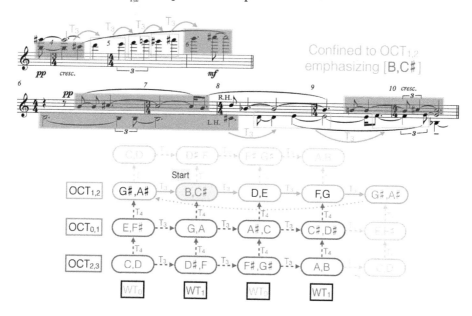

A brief reference to $OCT_{0,1}$ follows.

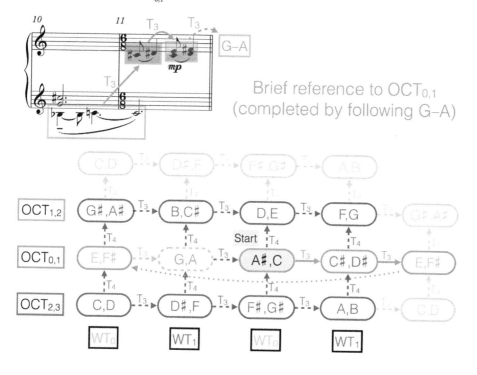

The passage then concludes with a full ascent through WT_1 in parallel 4s, accompanied with three additional 2s. Two of these belong to WT_1, and one of them does not (C-D).

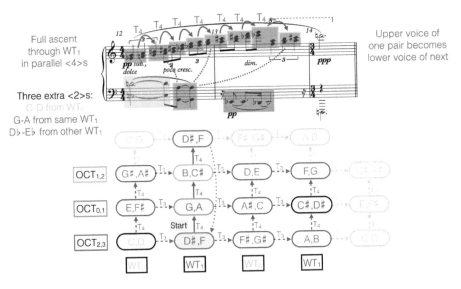

The final cadence on D represents a return to the first measure of the passage, where D-F♯ momentarily suggested D as a centric tone. Locally, it also gives the briefest echo of a traditional V–I cadence: the cadential D is preceded by A-C♯ in the upper strand ($\hat{5}$ and $\hat{7}$ in D major?) and by E♭ and D♭ in the lower strand ($♭\hat{2}$ and $\hat{7}$ in D major?).

27

John Adams, *On the Transmigration of Souls* (2002)

This work memorializes those killed in the destruction of the World Trade Center in the 9/11 attacks in New York. It is a large oratorio for orchestra, chorus, children's choir, and a pre-recorded tape. The work opens with a duet for sopranos and altos, singing an untexted vocalise. The voices move in rhythmic unison and the interval between them is always a perfect fifth. The passage as a whole uses nine of the twelve possible perfect fifths, numbered in the order in which they first occur. The slowly moving perfect fifths give the music a haunted, sorrowful quality—all the brightness and brilliance has been leached out, and we are in a musical world of unornamented grey. Over this solemn incantation, voices are heard (not shown here) speaking the names of the missing and the dead.

The motion from fifth to fifth is usually smooth—typically the fifths are a small interval apart (1, 2, 3, or 4 semitones). Until the last phrase, the larger intervals are always ascending and followed by a relatively smooth descent, following a traditional melodic rhetoric expressive of sorrow, and here suggestive of the ashes falling from the ruin of the towers.

The Art of Post-Tonal Analysis. Joseph N. Straus, Oxford University Press. © Joseph N. Straus 2022.
DOI: 10.1093/oso/9780197543979.003.0027

With the recurrence of these intervals between the fifths, we also get recurrences of the resulting tetrachord-types, and these tend to occur in certain favored pitch locations.

Beyond the recurring tetrachords, the music tends to coalesce into certain familiar collections, especially hexatonic and diatonic hexachords. One can think of these tetrachords and larger collections as primary building blocks, but it probably makes more sense to think of them as products of the various perfect fifths and their combinations. More specifically, one can think of the hexatonic and diatonic hexachords as transpositional combinations of (07) with some trichord or tetrachord.

To trace the movement of the perfect fifths through this passage it can be helpful to construct a musical space in which each perfect fifth is situated in proximity to fifths related by 1, 2, 3, or 4 semitones. The nine perfect fifths used in the piece are positioned so that moving up a column means T_4, moving right to left means T_2, moving SW to NE means T_1, and moving SE to NW means T_3. Note that all of these transpositions are in pitch space. The larger collections emerge from these motions, with hexatonic collections in the columns, diatonic collections in the rows, and octatonic collections (which do not play much of a role in the passage) in the NW-SE diagonals.

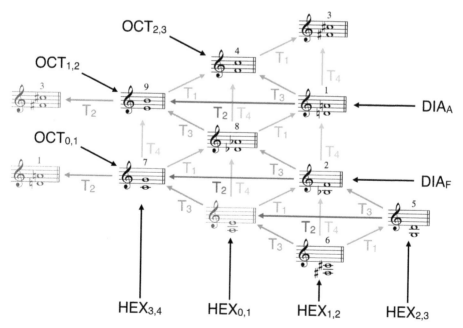

One can hear the phrases of the music, designated by the composer with articulation marks and a retaking of breath, as movements within this space. The first three phrases are confined to the central spine of the space.

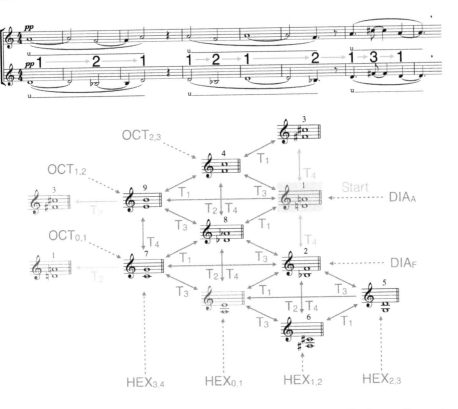

The next group of phrases traces a generally symmetrical, generally descending pattern toward the bottom of the space, weaving around the central spine.

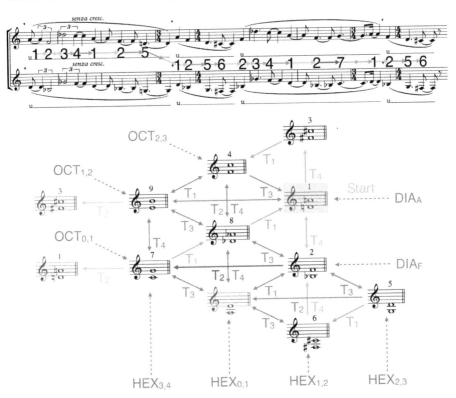

The final group of phrases has somewhat more complex motions through the space, but generally downward around the central spine, until a surprising upward surge at the end, simultaneously closing off this section of the music and opening out to the music, and the sorrows, that lie ahead.

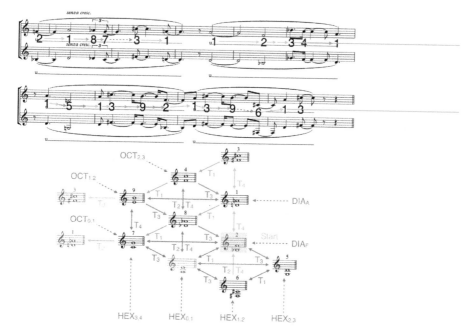

28

Sofia Gubaidulina, *Reflections on the Theme* B–A–C–H (2002)

This passage contains three distinct musical materials: widely spaced statements of (026); a chromatic melody within a very narrow compass of a whole tone; and a double canon in inversion in the style of J.S. Bach. Despite their obvious contrast, these three types of music have subtle affinities and suggest the possibility of a reconciliation toward which the work as a whole strives.

The Art of Post-Tonal Analysis. Joseph N. Straus, Oxford University Press. © Joseph N. Straus 2022.
DOI: 10.1093/oso/9780197543979.003.0028

Let's consider first the (026) strand. Within this strand, the aggregate of all twelve notes is presented as a series partitioned into four discrete forms of (026). The first two trichords are related at T_5, as are the last two. The middle two trichords are related at I_1 (in order), as are the first and last.

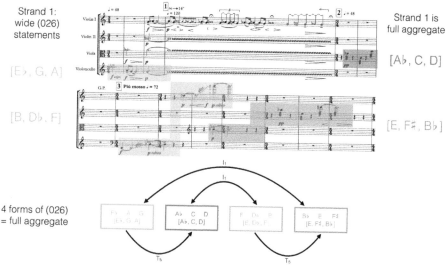

Is there any hint of the BACH theme referred to in the work's title (i.e., B♭–A–C–B) in this network of (026)? One can imagine the (026) network as an array, with (026) in the columns and (0123) in the rows. One of those rows contains a rotation of B♭-A-C-B. One of the rows of the array—E♭-D-D♭-E—is isolated in register; the other two rows are dispersed across the registers. In this way, we get a slight hint of BACH. The reference is somewhat buried here, but becomes explicit later in the piece.

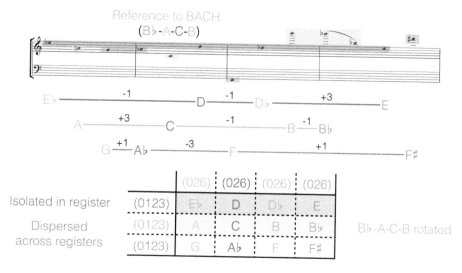

		(026)	(026)	(026)	(026)	
Isolated in register	(0123)	E♭	D	D♭	E	
Dispersed	(0123)	A	C	B	B♭	B♭-A-C-B rotated
across registers	(0123)	G	A♭	F	F♯	

The chromatic melody contains only three different pitches—G, A♭, and A—and presents them mostly in a fixed order, as a recurring four-note series: A-G-A♭-G.

Strand 2: chromatic melody

Only 3 pitches: G, A♭, A

Alternating G - A♭   Four-note series: A - G - A♭ - G

The chromatic melody bears an intimate relationship to the (026) network. Specifically, it fills in and animates the whole-tone G-A within the first (026). Its central tone, A♭, reinforced and sustained in second violin and viola, then becomes the first note of the second (026).

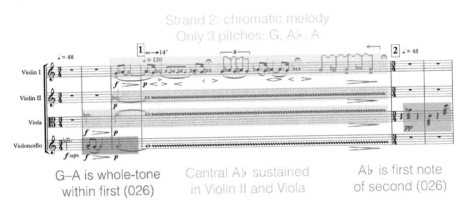

Strand 2: chromatic melody
Only 3 pitches: G, A♭, A

G–A is whole-tone   Central A♭ sustained   A♭ is first note
within first (026)   in Violin II and Viola   of second (026)

The four notes heard in the passage so far (E♭-G-A as the first (026) and G-A♭-A as the chromatic melody) together form (0126): [E♭, G, A♭, A]. Other members of the same set class can be heard in the interstices of the (026) network. Within the four (026), each whole-tone is filled in chromatically by a nearby note, creating a network of (0126) that is isographic with the previously discussed network of (026).

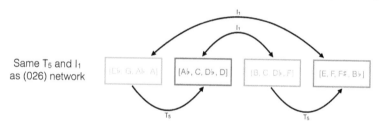

Each whole-tone in (026) filled chromatically by nearby note

The music that follows is a double canon in inversion. The four voices enter at a rhythmic distance of two quarter notes. The lower canon, between cello and viola, is at the octave. The upper canon, which is the strict pitch inversion of the lower one, is at the unison between the two violins.

Strand 3: inverted double canon

Lower canon
at the octave

Unison upper canon
at strict pitch inversion

The leading canonic voice (in the cello) is taken almost literally from Bach's *Art of Fugue*. This is the moment in that titanic work when the B–A–C–H subject is first introduced and combined with the original fugue subject. These are also the final measures Bach composed before his death. Gubaidulina extracts the countersubject as a melody for the cello, transposing it up a step to E minor.

In a Bach-like gesture, but without much concern for the resulting counterpoint, the viola imitates the cello in canon at the octave. This duet is full of dissonances that violate the norms of tonal counterpoint. The canon (at the unison) in the two violins similarly violates the norms of tonal counterpoint with its insistent, unresolved dissonances. The resulting four-voice passage evokes Bach in both the material (the countersubject from *Art of Fugue*) and its imitative, contrapuntal treatment. But the harmonic effect is highly dissonant and atonal—a chromatic wash in which all twelve pitch classes (excepting only C) are present.

Dissonances that violate tonal counterpoint

While the lower canon conveys an odd sort of E minor, the upper canon conveys mostly A major harmony (as V of D minor). These two canons are related by inversion around the E they share. Within this scheme, the E minor triad outlined in the lower duet is related by inversion to the A major triad outlined in the upper duet. We can think of the relations among the four canonic tunes in their instrumental network in very much the same way we thought of the relationship between the (026) and the (0126) within their pitch-class networks.

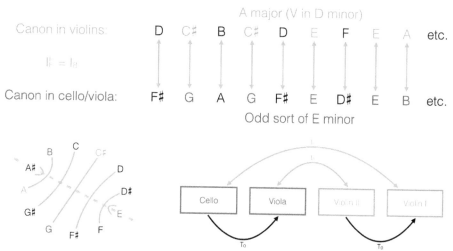

Within the double canon, a network of (013) trichords shapes the structure in ways that also resonate with the (026), (0126), and instrumental networks. With its inversional symmetry and network formation, the Bach-like material thus shares a deep affinity with the earlier (026)-based material.

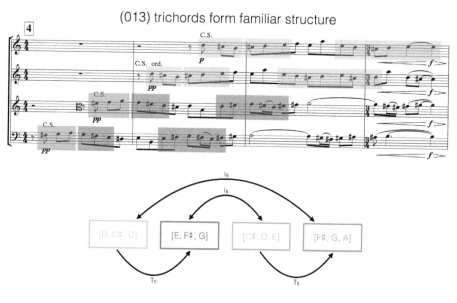

The three basic sorts of musical material in this work—the (026) network, the chromatic melody, and the quotations and paraphrases from J.S. Bach—come together in the brief chorale that concludes the work. The first violin gives a straightforward presentation of the B–A–C–H cypher: B♭–A–C–B. The B–A–C–H cypher is accompanied in parallel motion four semitones lower in the second violin and in an ascending chromatic line in the viola. Each of the upper strings thus projects a form of the chromatic tetrachord (0123). The chords formed between the upper three parts are all major or minor triads: G♭ major, D minor, A♭ major, and E minor. These triads pair into complementary hexatonic collections and together form the aggregate of all twelve tones. The upper three parts can thus be thought of in virtually the same way we thought of the (026) network at the beginning of the piece: an array with (0123) in the rows and, in this case, (037) rather than (026) in the columns. And what of the cello part, slightly misaligned beneath the homorhythmic upper parts? It refers directly back to the (026) strand with which the work began: [E♭, G, A], the first three notes of the piece, to which A♭ is adjoined, creating (0126). Its concluding A♭ dissonates the final E minor triad, just as its previous notes dissonate the other triads. The concluding chorale thus represents a moment of historical and stylistic reconciliation, between the (026) network, the chromatic melody, and the direct and indirect references to *Art of Fugue*, and between Bach and Gubaidulina.

(026)-network, chromatic melody, and J.S. Bach quotes combined

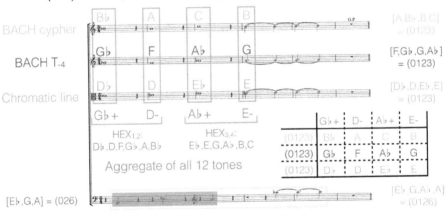

Cello notes dissonate each triad

29

Thomas Adès, *The Tempest*, Act III, Scene 5 (2003)

This passage comes near the beginning of the concluding scene of *The Tempest* by Thomas Adès, based on Shakespeare's play by the same name. At this point in the opera, all of the human characters have departed, headed back home to Italy. Ariel, the "airy spirit" of the island, who had been acting as a servant to Prospero, has been set free. She sings her pleasure in an extraordinarily high vocal register to an untexted vocalise whose vowels are the vowels of her name: a—i—e. The music is an ecstatic celebration of freedom, soaring off into the stratosphere, amid rapidly ascending and slowly descending accompanying lines.

The vocal line alternates two intervals: 2 and 7. The interval 2 is always represented as two ascending semitones. The interval 7 is represented either by seven semitones ascending or, more commonly, five semitones descending.

If you alternate intervals 7 and 2, you will end up back at your starting point after passing through 7 additional notes. The eight notes of this combination cycle amount to an eight-note series for this melody. The melody states the series two

The Art of Post-Tonal Analysis. Joseph N. Straus, Oxford University Press. © Joseph N. Straus 2022.
DOI: 10.1093/oso/9780197543979.003.0029

times in order, and begins a third statement. To put it another way, the melody moves around the cycle two complete times, and then starts a third time.

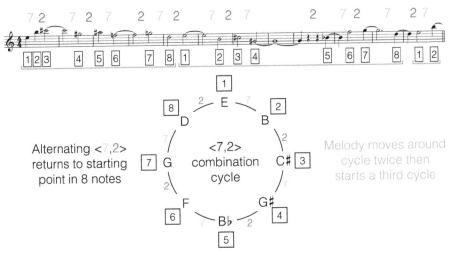

The three-note segments of this cycle are all members of set class (025). In fact, the music alternates inversionally related members of that set class: first (025), then (035), and so on. What we have here is an RI-chain, where the last two notes in one link become the first two notes in the next link. The links in the chain are related by inversion around the two notes they share.

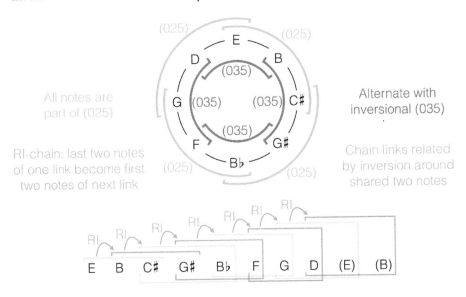

In addition to the regularities of interval and pitch, there is also a rhythmic pattern involved. Put crudely, the pattern is short-short-long, but usually the short notes last for four eighth notes and the long notes last for eight eighth notes. So we have a recurring pattern of 4+4+8. In the first part of the melody, this pattern lines up pretty well with the written bar lines, but in the second part of the melody, the pattern starts one quarter note too late, and the melody is syncopated against the bar line. The pitch pattern and the rhythm pattern interact in complicated ways. The pitches repeat every eight notes. The rhythm pattern (short-short-long) repeats every three notes. As a result, the two patterns are always out of phase with each other, at least in this passage.

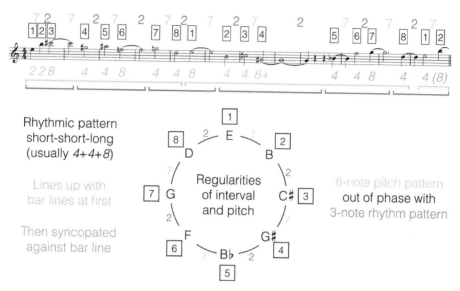

The accompaniment consists of two additional lines, a bass and an upper voice. Let's look first at the bass. In its pitches, the bass follows the same <7, 2> compound cycle as the vocal line, but backwards, or counterclockwise. It uses the same eight pitches as the vocal melody, but presents them in the opposite order. All of the things we said about the vocal melody—about its intervals and its three-note segments—are true of the bass also, but in reverse order. The bass line moves relentlessly downward. But when it gets to a very low D♭, it bounces up three octaves, and resumes its descent.

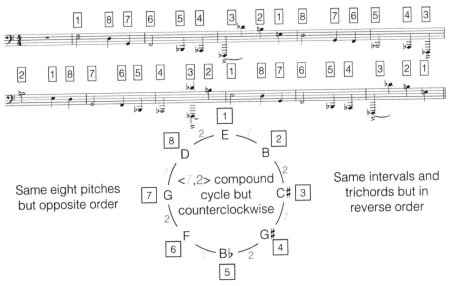

As for its rhythms, the bass uses a pattern of two shorts and a long, just like the vocal melody, but does it twice as fast. Counting in eighth notes, the vocal melody goes 8-4-4, 8-4-4, while the bass goes 4-2-2, 4-2-2. And while the vocal melody was somewhat free in deploying this pattern, the bass is absolutely strict. As a result, the vocal melody and the bass are in a kind of diminution canon, with the bass moving through its pitches twice as fast as the vocal melody. In this passage, the vocal melody cycles around the circle twice in a clockwise direction, while the bass cycles around the circle four times in a counterclockwise direction.

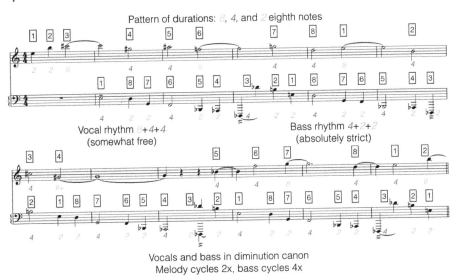

Vocals and bass in diminution canon
Melody cycles 2x, bass cycles 4x

The inner voice is organized in a similar way. Its pitches move clockwise around the circle. In each trip around the circle, the pitches get higher and higher until they reach a very high C♯—the third pitch on the clock face—when they jump down three octaves and start ascending again. It's just the opposite of the bass, which moved down to a low C♯ before jumping up. Because of the aligned rhythmic patterns in these two parts, the bass always reaches its low C♯ right around the moment when the inner voice reaches its high C♯.

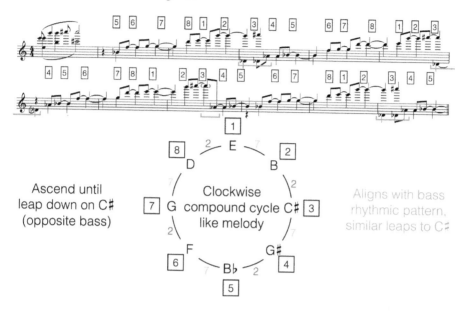

The rhythm of the inner voice is also patterned. Counting in eighth notes, the pattern is 1-2-5. Like the rhythms of the vocal melody and bass, this is a three-note rhythmic pattern, and thus does not align with the 8-note pitch pattern. Rhythmically, however, it repeats every eight eighth-notes, and thus always occurs in the same place within each measure. In that respect, it is like the bass rhythm which also lasts for eight eighth-notes, and thus also occurs in the same position within each measure.

Sum of 8 eighths
fits the meter
(just like the bass)

Rhythmic pattern
of *1* + *2* + *5* eighths

3-note rhythm pattern
doesn't align with
8-note pitch pattern

Adding the introductory first measure into the mix, we have what appears to be a pretty complicated situation: three independent lines, each with its own pitch pattern and rhythm pattern. Within each line, the pitch and rhythm patterns do not align. And yet the overall impression of the music is of something relatively simple and harmonically motionless, as though one single thing is happening, rather than lots of different things happening at the same time.

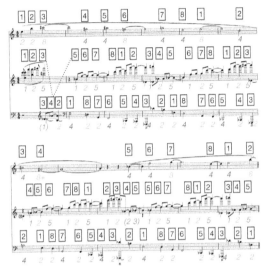

Melody
Clockwise pitch pattern
Rhythm *8+4+4*
Begins aligned w/meter
Ends in conflict w/meter

Inner Voice
Clockwise pitch pattern
Always ascending
Rhythm *1+2+5*
Consistent offset from meter

Bass
Counterclockwise pitch pattern
Always descending
Rhythm *4+2+2*
Strictly aligned with meter

I think there are two main reasons for that sense of simplicity and stasis. The first reason is that, amid all of this activity, only eight notes are involved. We hear them in different orders, and at different rates of speed, and in different, registers, but still there are only eight notes. These eight notes comprise one of the three octatonic collections, that familiar scale of alternating semitones and whole tones.

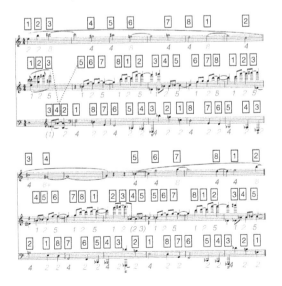

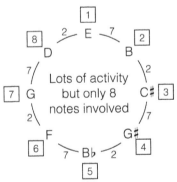

Different orders, different rates, different registers, but just simple octatonic collection:

$$\overset{1}{E}\overset{2}{F}\overset{1}{G}\overset{2}{G\sharp}\overset{1}{B\flat}\overset{2}{B}\overset{1}{C\sharp}\overset{2}{D}(E)$$

The second reason has to do with the three-note groups. As we noted earlier, every three-note melodic segment is a member of set class (025). The same trichord type is formed again and again *between* the parts. I have used boxes to identify just a few of the many such instances. As a result, there is a high degree of harmonic uniformity in the passage, with all of the three-note melodic segments and very many of the three-note harmonies representing the same set type. This astonishingly high degree of melodic, rhythmic, and harmonic patterning creates a paradoxical effect. Because there are so many different and nonaligned patterns involved, no one pattern predominates, and indeed the sense of patterning recedes, and we get an impression of a freely improvised swirl, a joyous cacophony that corresponds well with Ariel's state of mind.

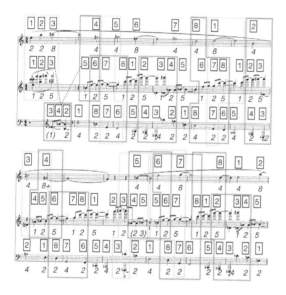

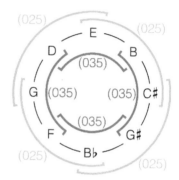

Every trichord segment is member of (025) or (035)

Harmonic uniformity between all 3-note melodic segments and many 3-note harmonies

30

Thomas Adès, "Days," from *Four Quarters* for string quartet (2010)

This passage is composed in three layers: 1) an ostinato on C♯ in the second violin, 2) a note-against-note duet in first violin and viola, and 3) an additional counterpoint in the cello.

C♯ ostinato in second violin

Duet in first violin and viola

Counterpoint in cello

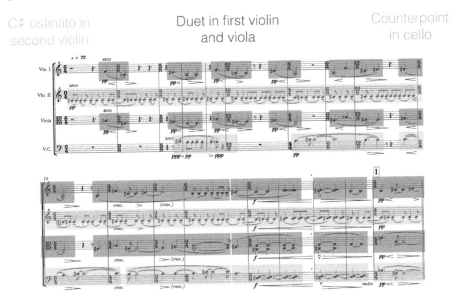

The ostinato on C♯ follows a nine-note rhythmic pattern: 1-1-2-1-2-1-2-1-2 (counted in eighth notes). Its total duration is thirteen eighth-notes, so it virtually never aligns with a notated downbeat. It is heard eleven times in the passage (including a partial statement toward the end), and has the effect of a slightly irregular heartbeat.

The Art of Post-Tonal Analysis. Joseph N. Straus, Oxford University Press. © Joseph N. Straus 2022.
DOI: 10.1093/oso/9780197543979.003.0030

Rhythmic pattern: 1-1-2-1-2-1-2-1-2

Duration thirteen eighth notes, rarely aligns with downbeat

Pattern heard eleven times

C♯ ostinato in second violin

(partial)

Has the effect of a slightly irregular heartbeat

The note-against-note duet involves seven different dyads. The dyads are usually formed between the first violin and viola, occasionally doubled by either the ostinato C♯ in the second violin or one of the notes in the additional line in the cello. But sometimes the situation is a bit more complicated, with a note left over from a previous dyad, or other instrumental complications—dyad 5 is particularly vulnerable in this way. As a progression of dyads, there are basically four gestures in the passage and the beginning of a fifth, each beginning with dyad 1 and progressing in a (mostly) orderly way through the remaining dyads.

Duet involves seven dyads

mm. 1–4
dyads 1-2-3-4

mm. 5–8
1-2-3-4-5

mm. 8–10
1-2-(5)-3-4-5

mm. 11–17
1-2-(5)-3-4-5-6-"7"

The dyads originate in a layered presentation of two compound interval cycles: <6, 4> and <8, 2>. The whole pattern would involve twelve dyads before returning to its starting point, but the music uses only the first seven dyads. The intervals within the dyads are always 7 or 5.

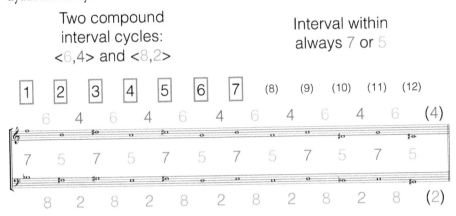

Each line traverses one of the two whole-tone scales twice. The whole complex involves a sequential pattern in which a pair of dyads is transposed down two semitones each time.

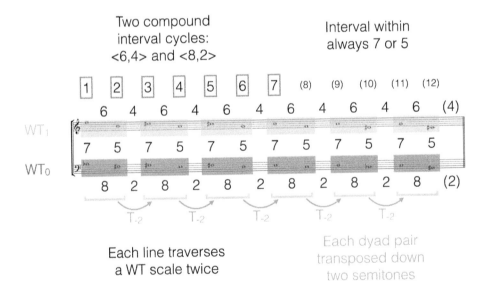

Each line traverses
a WT scale twice

Each dyad pair
transposed down
two semitones

As noted, the music uses only the first seven dyads of the array. The fifth dyad is problematic in the music because its C♯ simply doubles the ostinato tone. In response, the music often retains A from the fourth dyad. The seventh dyad (E-B) is represented by B alone, without its partner, E.

Until virtually the end of the passage, the third strand of the music—the additional counterpoint in the cello—contains only three different notes. Its C♯ doubles the ostinato tone. Its B♭ often doubles a tone of one of the dyads. Its B♮ is harder to digest, and is probably best understood as a representative of dyad 7 (E-B).

The dyads are heard in conjunction with the ostinato C♯, resulting in a progression of six trichords. The first five are members of (037) or (027), which can be thought of as the dyadic perfect fifth together with either an added third or an added whole-tone. The sixth and final trichord is (016)—a perfect fifth plus a semitone. This represents a dissonation and intensification of the harmony, as well as a cadential coagulation that marks the end of the first section of music.

31

Caroline Shaw, *Valencia* for string quartet (2012)

This is the opening passage of a work intended, in the composer's words, as "an untethered embrace of the architecture of the common Valencia orange, through billowing harmonics and somewhat viscous chords and melodies." The piece presents a musical surface that is bright and vividly colored, a focused swirl of energetic activity. In the upper instruments, we hear two different patterns of oscillating string harmonics, each lasting for roughly half of the passage. Beneath the harmonics, we hear a pizzicato line in the cello (played twice), a progression of arpeggiated major and minor triads, and finally a cadential progression directed toward an A major triad, where the subsequent section begins.

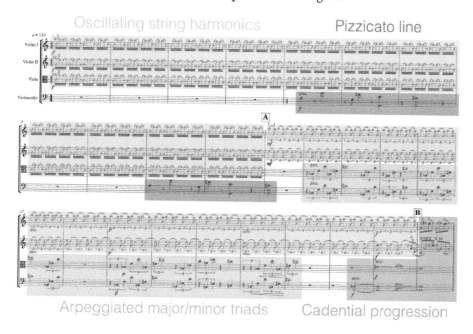

The opening music, a sort of vamp, involves the rapid alternation of two chords: G-D-A and A-E-B. Vertically, both chords are arranged as a stack of perfect fifths, with A at the top of the first stack and at the bottom of the second stack. Each instrumental voice moves up and down by two semitones: G-A, D-E, and A-B. The collection is symmetrical on A. Taken as a whole, the five sounding notes comprise a pentatonic scale, G-A-B-D-E, although without making clear which might be scale

The Art of Post-Tonal Analysis. Joseph N. Straus, Oxford University Press. © Joseph N. Straus 2022.
DOI: 10.1093/oso/9780197543979.003.0031

degree $\hat{1}$. Both G (the lowest note) and A (the highest note) would seem to be good candidates.

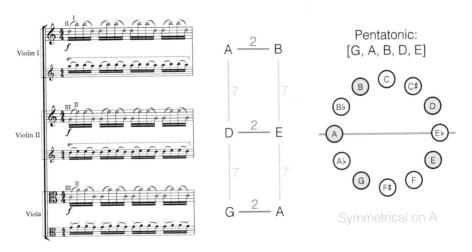

Beneath this shimmering vamp, the cello provides a pizzicato line of two single notes, two dyads, and a three-note chord. It reinforces our sense that the pentatonic collection is symmetrical around A. A is embellished by a lower neighbor G, replicating at that level the rapid alternation of G and A in the viola. The three-measure phrase concludes with what sounds like a cadential progression in A major, from the subtonic triad (G major) to the tonic triad (A major).

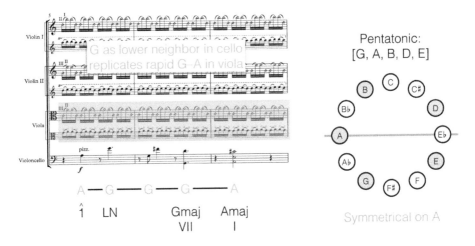

This cadential arrival affirms A as scale-degree î of the pentatonic collection in the upper voices: A-B-D-E-G-A. The A is thus the principal tone, both as scale-degree î and as an inversional center. The cello also introduces two new notes, F♯ and C♯, thus expanding the prevailing collection from pentatonic on A to Mixolydian on A: A-B-C♯-D-E-F♯-G-A. The expansion entails a shift in the inversional axis, from inversion around A to inversion around E.

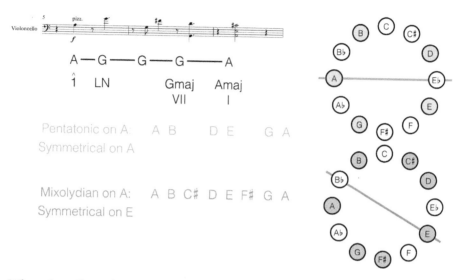

When the cello melody ends, a new oscillation of string harmonics begins in the two violins. It lies within the original pentatonic collection, but its orientation has shifted from A to E, confirming that shift in the previous music. Vertically, both chords are arranged as perfect fifths, with E on the bottom of the first dyad and on top of the second one. Each instrumental voice moves up and down by five semitones: E-A and B-E.

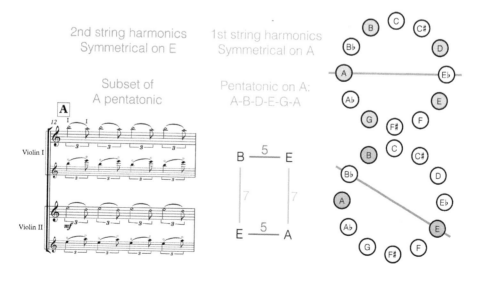

Beneath this new shimmering oscillation, we hear arpeggiated major and minor triads in the cello and viola. For the first group of chords, the instruments are playing in octaves. In the second group of chords, the instruments are playing in canon at the octave, with the viola one quarter-note triplet behind the cello. The triads are still there, but slightly disjointed.

Arpeggiated triads in cello and viola

First time in octaves   Then disjointed canon

Ab+   A-   A+   Bb-   Bb+   B-   B+

The basis for this arrangement of triads is a seven-chord segment of the SLIDE-P chain. The cello and viola start their melodies on Bb major, halfway through this progression on Bb major, then play through the whole progression from the beginning. starting on Ab major, alternating SLIDE and P until an arrival on B major, the goal of the progression. Unlike the pentatonic and diatonic first half of the passage, this progression is highly chromatic, and uses eleven of the twelve notes: only G is missing.

Full aggregate
(except G)

Goal of the
progression

The missing G arrives in the final measures of the passage, as part of a cadential progression directed toward the A major triad. In these measures, there is a symmetrical convergence on A: from B a step above—B was the goal of the SLIDE-P chain in the preceding passage—and from G a step below. A sense of symmetrical balance on A has been part of the music from the very beginning, so this arrival on A simultaneously initiates a new section of the music and recalls the music's point of departure.

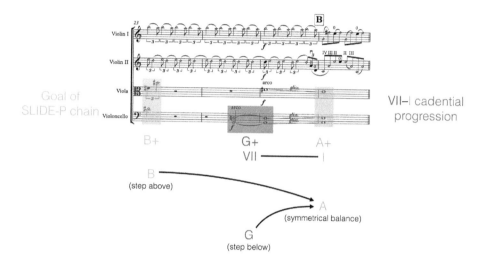

32

Chen Yi, *Energetic Duo* for two
violins (2015)

This passage represents exactly three-fifths of the whole work from which it is extracted. It consists of three thirteen-measure periods (labeled I–III); the remainder of the piece (not shown) consists of two additional thirteen measure periods. Each period is divided into four small sections, each with a duration of thirteen quarter notes. Each of these smaller thirteen-beat sections uses a consistent rotation of three contrasting types of musical material, labeled X, Y, and Z.

Three 13-measure periods to begin (I, II, III)
Each period = 4 sections with duration of 13 quarter notes
Each section = 3 types of material in the same order (X, Y, Z)

In the first period, X is a harmonic dyad; in the second period, X expands to a four-note chord; in the third period, X is a melody in eighth notes. In the first and second periods, Y is a four-note chord; in the third period, Y shrinks to a harmonic dyad. In all three periods, Z is a dissonant tremolo.

The Art of Post-Tonal Analysis. Joseph N. Straus, Oxford University Press. © Joseph N. Straus 2022.
DOI: 10.1093/oso/9780197543979.003.0032

Characteristics of the material in the different periods

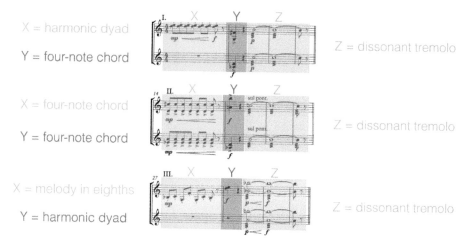

Over the course of each period, X shrinks in number of attacks, Y expands, and Z stays the same (the number of attacks is shown in parentheses).

Differences in the number of attacks:
X shrinks, Y expands, Z stays the same

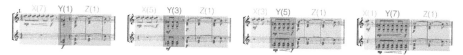

This careful formal arrangement gives the impression of something static, rigid, and mechanical, but the effect of the music is quite different: playful, capricious, bursting with energy. That has to do in part with the sheer level of activity—mostly eighth notes and rapid tremolos—but it also reflects shifting contrasts and affinities in the pitch organization.

Differences in the number of attacks:
X shrinks, Y expands, Z stays the same

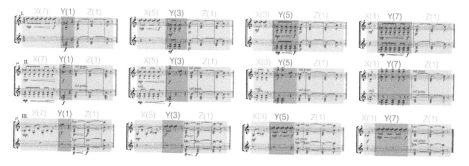

X, Y, and Z give an initial impression of maximum distinctiveness and contrast. X is a repeated major second, played in staccato eighth notes over a crescendo. Y is a single four-note chord, played forte. Z is a minor second, played in a soft tremolo. But there are audible points of affinity among them. X and Y share a common tone: D. Y contains a major second (like X) and two minor seconds (like Z).

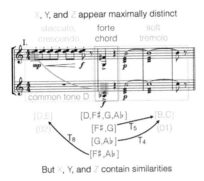

But X, Y, and Z contain similarities

As the piece progresses, these sorts of subtle affinities are emphasized and the musical materials become more like each other, to the extent of changing places. X is always first, Y second, and Z third, but their internal characters adapt to each other, and take on new identities. In the first period, X wanes while Y waxes, but all three elements are fixed in pitch. In the second period, Z continues unchanged, but both X and Y are derived from the original Y. Most significantly, X is now the exact pitch transposition of what Y was: X has become Y. What is more, the dyad [D,E] that comprised the original X, now in the second period reappears within the temporal span of Y. In these ways, the identities of X and Y become enmeshed. In the third period, the transformations continue. X is now a melody. Y consists entirely of the dyad [D,E], which was X in the first period: Y has become X. Z is still a tremolo, but shifted in register and with an additional note added. Z was [B,C]; now it is [A,B♭,B], a chromatic trichord that recalls the chromatic trichord embedded in the original Y: Z has become Y.

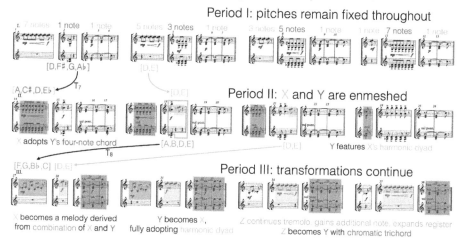

Amid the fragmentation and the evident contrast among the elements, they are nonetheless bound together in a network of affinities and transformations. Common tones connect the disparate units. [D,E] in the initial X returns as the terminal Y. The tritone [A♭,D] at the bottom of the four-note chord in the initial Y returns at the bottom of the contrasting four-chord in the subsequent Y. [A,B] at the top of the second Y returns in the final statement of Z. The note B♭, the last of the twelve tones to appear in the final X returns, doubled at the octave, at the top of the final Z. In all of these ways, the contrasting components are linked together.

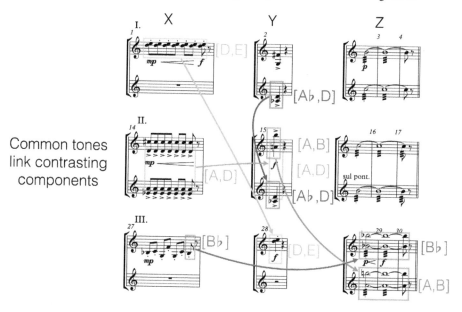

A more subtle affinity among the contrasting components involves the perfect fourth/fifth and especially the gesture of transposition at T_5 or T_7. Within the components, one often finds the interval of the perfect fourth/fifth.

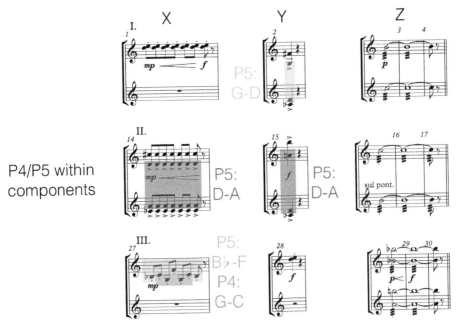

Between the components, the same interval is used as a way of transposing semitones, whole-tones, or an entire four-note chord. Through its radical and mechanistic formal fragmentation, this passage raises questions of musical unity—is it possible to bind such disparate fragments together? To bring them into meaningful relationship with each other? The answers in this case have to do with the shifting identities of the fragments, their shared content, and the transformations that bind them.

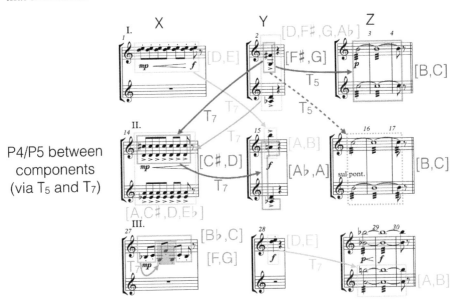

33

Suzanne Farrin, "Unico spirto,"
from *Dolce la morte* (2016)

This is the first of a cycle of songs based on the love poetry of Michelangelo. It takes as its text five lines from the middle of a longer poem: a four-line stanza and the first line of the next stanza. This is a passionate though bewildered cry of love and longing: the poet sees his lover as a godlike figure, who causes lovesickness (a sort of death) but doesn't feel it himself; who is free but ensnares the poet's heart; who is loving, but causes pain. The poet wonders how so beautiful a face can cause such un-beautiful effects, but the text breaks off before this final paradox can be explored.

> *Unico spirto e da me solo inteso*
> *che non ha morte e morte altrui procaccia*
> *veggio e truovo chi, sciolto, 'l cor m'allaccia*
> *e da chi giova sol mi sento offeso.*
>   *Com'esser può, signor, che d'un bel volto*

> Unique spirit, understood by me alone,
> Who cannot die and yet causes death to others,
> I see one who, although free, shackles my heart
> And though he offers help, I feel only pain.
>   How can it be, lord, that from a beautiful face…

The musical setting of this poetic fragment consists of fourteen musical fragments (identified by letters in the score). It is scored for countertenor, oboe, and bassoon, with the bass entering quietly at the end with a crucial pitch. The music unfolds slowly and as though in a dream, with long sustained notes (often elaborated by trills or pitch-bending). There are no bar lines and any sense of meter is fleeting at best. The tempo marking is "*molto flessible e rubato*, floating, with brief articulations of pulse."

The Art of Post-Tonal Analysis. Joseph N. Straus, Oxford University Press. © Joseph N. Straus 2022.
DOI: 10.1093/oso/9780197543979.003.0033

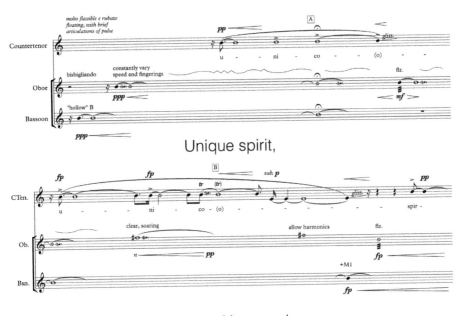

Unique spirit,

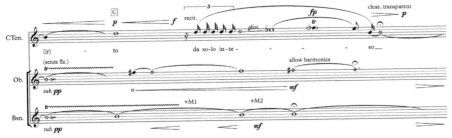

understood by me alone,

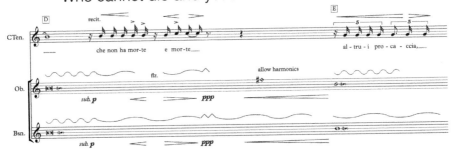

Who cannot die and yet causes death to others,

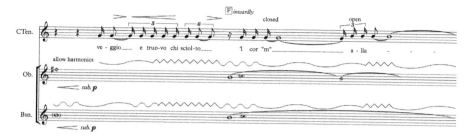

I see one who, although free, shackles my heart

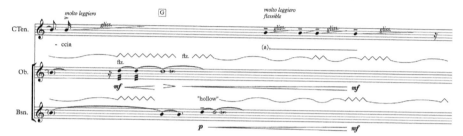

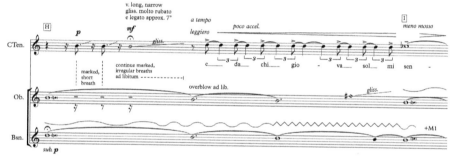

And though he offers help, I feel only pain.

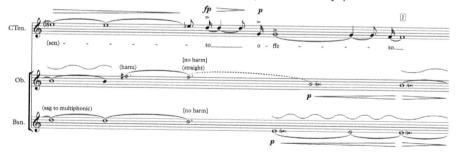

How can it be, lord, that from a beautiful face…

The music begins with the B above middle C in various articulations. It is soon surrounded by F♯, seven semitones above (A fragment), and E, seven semitones below (B fragment.

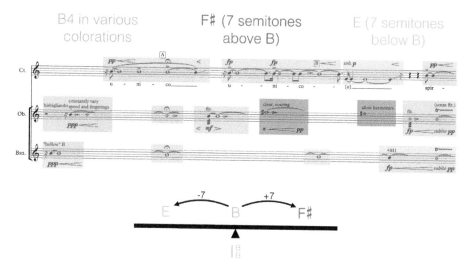

With that inversional axis in mind, the arrival of D at the beginning of the C fragment suggests a motion toward G♯, its inversional partner, and the arrival of D♯ a moment later suggests a motion toward G[natural], its inversional partner. These expected inversional partners arrive in due course. In the meantime, however, the D and D♯ suggest another inversional axis: they are inversional partners within the B-F♯ perfect fifth. Indeed, we can hear the motion from D to D♯ as motivated by the search for D's inversional partner with respect to B-F♯. At the same time, the D and D♯ create B minor and B major triads, related by P. In a moment, we will hear other triads that also contain B, the foundational pitch class.

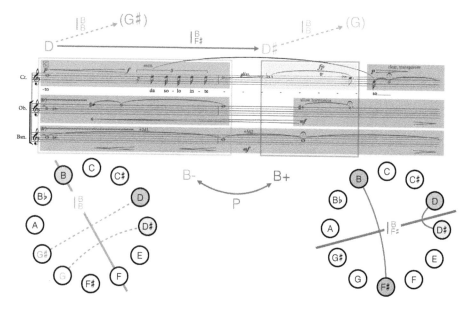

The introduction of G (in the E fragment) suggests new triadic possibilities. Initially, we might take it as part of an E minor triad, but the arrival of D a moment later seems to affirm a G major triad. All of the triads so far can be located on an LPR-cycle, which connects via minimal voice leading all six triads that share B as a common tone. The piece has moved along this cycle from B minor and B major (for lines 1 and 2 of the poem) to E minor and G major (for line 3).

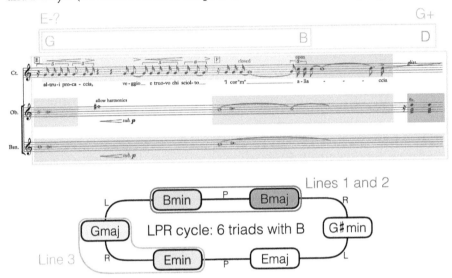

As the fourth poetic line draws to a close, the music returns to B minor and B major, but now they occur simultaneously rather than sequentially. The clash between D natural and D♯ is intense. We also get a hint of E minor, and the harmonic return of these triads marks the end of the poetic stanza. There is also a reaffirmation of the axes of symmetry that have grounded the harmonic and melodic activity so far: inversion around B and inversion within the perfect fifth B-F♯.

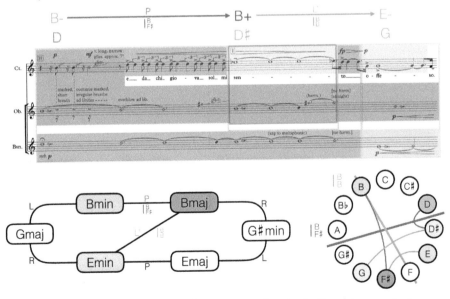

At this point, a new poetic stanza begins, one that is destined to remain incomplete, and the music likewise breaks out of its narrow, balanced sphere and enters a new melodic and harmonic space. The music moves outside the confines of the LPR cycle and asserts a new axis of inversional balance, on D-G♯. At the beginning of the new poetic line, the voice comes to rest on E, decorated by a neighbor note D. For the first time in the piece, the note B disappears, never to be heard again. The melody then settles on a now-stabilized D, beneath which, thanks to the quiet entrance of the bass, we hear two SLIDE-related triads, E major and F minor, sharing a triadic third, and intermingled. The E major triad belongs to the LPR cycle, but the F minor triad moves outside the cycle. The two triads are related by inversion around G♯. The melodic D represents the opposite end of that inversional axis.

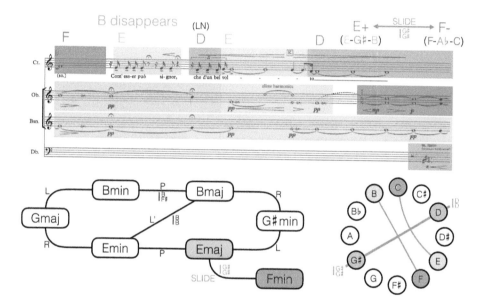

At the end of the song, we hear the same congealed SLIDE-related triads, E major and F minor. The melody's insistence on a stable-sounding D makes me want to hear one other triad, D minor. Like F minor, it lies outside the original LPR cycle and, also like F minor, it relates to a member of the circle by inversion around D-G♯.

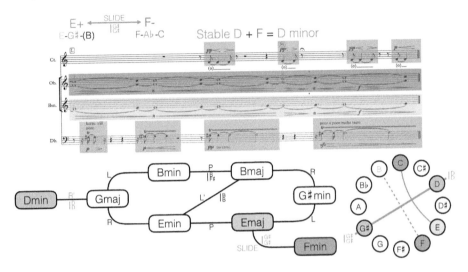

This song, a setting of a poetic fragment and the first in a long cycle, thus ends in an open way, having pushed outside of the musical boundaries it initially set for itself.

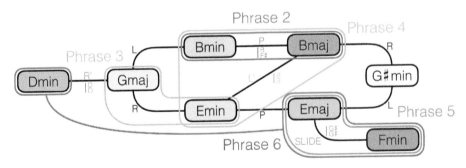

Post-Tonal Primer

Pitch and pitch class

A *pitch* is a specific point on the continuum of audible sound (the eighty-eight keys of the piano keyboard, for example, correspond to eighty-eight different pitches). A *pitch class* is group of pitches related by octave, and thus with the same (or enharmonic) name. There are twelve pitch classes, which can be visualized on the *pitch-class clock face*, where each pitch-class letter name is associated with a *pitch-class integer*, 0 to 11.

Pitch and pitch-class intervals (ordered and unordered)

A *pitch interval* is the number of semitones between two pitches. An *ordered pitch interval* identifies the number of semitones between the pitches *and* the direction (up or down) from the first note to the second (using plus and minus signs). An *unordered pitch interval* identifies the number of semitones alone, without regard to direction or which pitch comes first. A *pitch-class interval* is the number of semitones between two pitch classes. An *ordered pitch-class interval* identifies the number of semitones from one pitch class to another, calculated on the pitch-class clock face. Ordered pitch-class intervals are expressed as positive (clockwise) integers from 1 to 11. An *unordered pitch-class interval* (also known as an *interval class*) identifies the space between two pitch classes, calculated as the shortest distance between them on the pitch-class clock face. Ordered pitch-class intervals that sum to 12 belong to the same interval class.

The Art of Post-Tonal Analysis. Joseph N. Straus, Oxford University Press. © Joseph N. Straus 2022.
DOI: 10.1093/oso/9780197543979.003.0034

Example	Some Ordered Pitch Intervals	Ordered Pitch-Class Interval	Interval Class (Unordered Pitch-Class Interval)	Ordered Pitch-Class Interval	Some Ordered Pitch Intervals	Example
A–B♭	+1, −11 +13, −23	1	1	11	−1, +11 −13, +23	B♭–A
A–B	+2, −10 +14, −22	2	2	10	−2, +10 −14, +22	B–A
A–C	+3, −9 +15, −21	3	3	9	−3, +9 −15, +21	C–A
A–C♯	+4, −8 +16, −20	4	4	8	−4, +8 −16, +20	C♯–A
A–D	+5, −7 +17, −19	5	5	7	−5, +7 −17, +19	D–A
A–E♭	+6, −6 +18, −18	6	6	6	−6, +6 −18, +18	E♭–A

Pitch-class sets

A *pitch-class set* is an unordered collection of pitch classes. We will mostly be concerned with two-note, three-note, and four-note sets (*dyads, trichords,* and *tetrachords*). Pitch-class sets are usually written in a compressed, scalar order called a *normal form*: the pitch classes are enclosed within square brackets, like [A, B♭, C♯] or [E, G♯, A, B♭].

Transposition (T_n)

Pitch-class sets are related by *transposition* (T) when each note in one set is transposed by the same *interval of transposition* (n) onto a corresponding note in another set. The interval of transposition is an ordered pitch-class interval. Transpositions are shown with an arrow labeled with the appropriate T_n. Transposition preserves the intervals in the set.

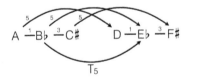
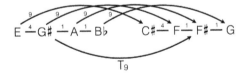

Inversion (I_n)

Pitch-class sets are related by *inversion* (I) when each note in one set is inverted by the same *index of inversion* (n) onto a corresponding note in another set. The index of inversion is the *sum* of the pitch-class integers of the corresponding notes (all sums are taken *mod 12*, i.e., subtract 12 from any number larger than 11). Inversions are shown with a doubled-headed arrow labeled with the appropriate I_n (the arrow is double-headed because inversion is its own inverse—doing it twice takes you back to your starting point). Inversion reverses the order of the intervals within the set.

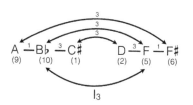
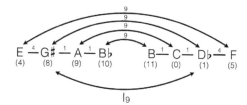

Inversion (I_Y^X)

Inversion can also be represented as I_Y^X where X and Y are pitch classes that invert onto each other (X and Y may be the same pitch class). There will be a number of possible names for each inversion—any pair of *inversional partners* will serve. Sets related by inversion will balance around an *inversional axis*.

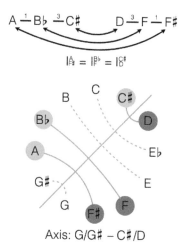
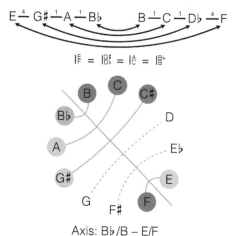

Axis: G/G♯ – C♯/D   Axis: B♭/B – E/F

Inversional symmetry

Some sets relate to themselves by inversion: they are *inversionally symmetrical.*

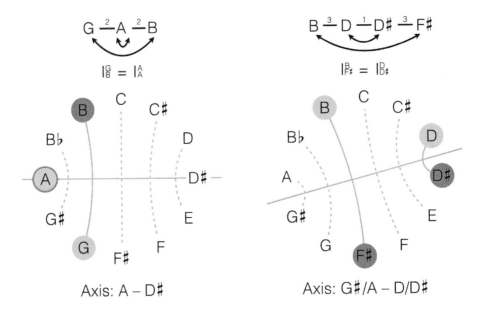

There are twelve different axes of inversion, corresponding to the twelve index numbers: I_0, I_1, I_2, and so on. Each inversion brings about a unique set of pairings of a note with an inversional partner.

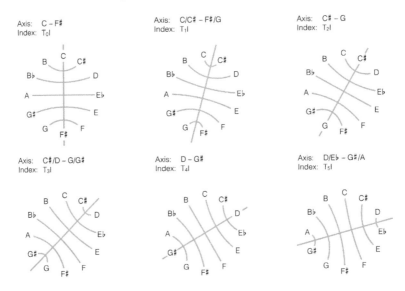

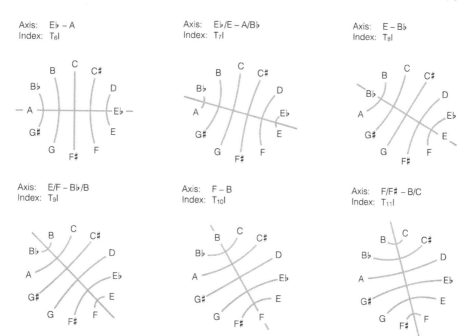

Axis: Eb – A
Index: T₆I

Axis: Eb/E – A/Bb
Index: T₇I

Axis: E – Bb
Index: T₈I

Axis: E/F – Bb/B
Index: T₉I

Axis: F – B
Index: T₁₀I

Axis: F/F# – B/C
Index: T₁₁I

Set class

Pitch-class sets related by transposition or inversion make up a *set class*. Set classes are named with their prime form, a string of numbers starting on 0 and enclosed in parentheses—for example, (025). There are six dyad classes (corresponding to the six interval classes), twelve trichord classes, and twenty-nine tetrachord classes, each with its own prime form. Because the analyses in this book are often focused on trichords, the twelve trichord-classes are listed here (every possible grouping of three notes belongs to one of them).

Prime Form	Representative Sets (Written in Normal Form Starting on C)
(012)	
(013)	
(014)	
(015)	
(016)	
(024)	
(025)	
(026)	
(027)	
(036)	
(037)	
(048)	

Transpositional combination (TC)

Sets that can be divided into two or more subsets related by transposition have the transpositional combination (TC) property. For sets with four notes or fewer, the TC property is notated with two numbers separated by an asterisk, like 3*4. That expression is read as either "two 3s related at T_4," or "two 4s related at T_3," both of which produce the tetrachord (0347). Here are all of the tetrachords with the TC property.

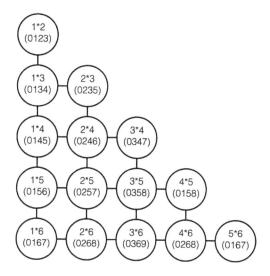

Referential collections

Diatonic (DIA). A diatonic collection is any transposition of the seven "white notes" of the piano. The diatonic collections can be identified by their key signature (e.g., $DIA_{1\sharp}$ or $DIA_{3\flat}$). If it is possible to ascertain a centric tone (scale degree $\hat{1}$), a diatonic collection can be ordered as one of the modes (e.g., Dorian, Phrygian, etc.).

Collection Name (Key Signature)	Ionian (Major) 2-2-1-2-2-2-1	Dorian 2-1-2-2-2-1-2	Phrygian 1-2-2-2-1-2-2	Lydian 2-2-2-1-2-2-1	Mixolydian 2-2-1-2-2-1-2	Aeolian (Minor) 2-1-2-2-1-2-2	Locrian 1-2-2-1-2-2-2
DIA0♮	C-D-E-F-G-A-B	D-E-F-G-A-B-C	E-F-G-A-B-C-D	F-G-A-B-C-D-E	G-A-B-C-D-E-F	A-B-C-D-E-F-G	B-C-D-E-F-G-A
DIA1♯	G-A-B-C-D-E-F♯	A-B-C-D-E-F♯-G	B-C-D-E-F♯-G-A	C-D-E-F♯-G-A-B	D-E-F♯-G-A-B-C	E-F♯-G-A-B-C-D	F♯-G-A-B-C-D-E
DIA2♯	D-E-F♯-G-A-B-C♯	E-F♯-G-A-B-C♯-D	F♯-G-A-B-C♯-D-E	G-A-B-C♯-D-E-F♯	A-B-C♯-D-E-F♯-G	B-C♯-D-E-F♯-G-A	C♯-D-E-F♯-G-A-B
DIA3♯	A-B-C♯-D-E-F♯-G♯	B-C♯-D-E-F♯-G♯-A	C♯-D-E-F♯-G♯-A-B	D-E-F♯-G♯-A-B-C♯	E-F♯-G♯-A-B-C♯-D	F♯-G♯-A-B-C♯-D-E	G♯-A-B-C♯-D-E-F♯
DIA4♯	E-F♯-G♯-A-B-C♯-D♯	F♯-G♯-A-B-C♯-D♯-E	G♯-A-B-C♯-D♯-E-F♯	A-B-C♯-D♯-E-F♯-G♯	B-C♯-D♯-E-F♯-G♯-A	C♯-D♯-E-F♯-G♯-A-B	D♯-E-F♯-G♯-A-B-C♯
DIA5♯	B-C♯-D♯-E-F♯-G♯-A♯	C♯-D♯-E-F♯-G♯-A♯-B	D♯-E-F♯-G♯-A♯-B-C♯	E-F♯-G♯-A♯-B-C♯-D♯	F♯-G♯-A♯-B-C♯-D♯-E	G♯-A♯-B-C♯-D♯-E-F♯	A♯-B-C♯-D♯-E-F♯-G♯
DIA6♯	F♯-G♯-A♯-B-C♯-D♯-E♯	G♯-A♯-B-C♯-D♯-E♯-F♯	A♯-B-C♯-D♯-E♯-F♯-G♯	B-C♯-D♯-E♯-F♯-G♯-A♯	C♯-D♯-E♯-F♯-G♯-A♯-B	D♯-E♯-F♯-G♯-A♯-B-C♯	E♯-F♯-G♯-A♯-B-C♯-D♯
DIA5♭	D♭-E♭-F-G♭-A♭-B♭-C	E♭-F-G♭-A♭-B♭-C-D♭	F-G♭-A♭-B♭-C-D♭-E♭	G♭-A♭-B♭-C-D♭-E♭-F	A♭-B♭-C-D♭-E♭-F-G♭	B♭-C-D♭-E♭-F-G♭-A♭	C-D♭-E♭-F-G♭-A♭-B♭
DIA4♭	A♭-B♭-C-D♭-E♭-F-G	B♭-C-D♭-E♭-F-G-A♭	C-D♭-E♭-F-G-A♭-B♭	D♭-E♭-F-G-A♭-B♭-C	E♭-F-G-A♭-B♭-C-D♭	F-G-A♭-B♭-C-D♭-E♭	G-A♭-B♭-C-D♭-E♭-F
DIA3♭	E♭-F-G-A♭-B♭-C-D	F-G-A♭-B♭-C-D-E♭	G-A♭-B♭-C-D-E♭-F	A♭-B♭-C-D-E♭-F-G	B♭-C-D-E♭-F-G-A♭	C-D-E♭-F-G-A♭-B♭	D-E♭-F-G-A♭-B♭-C
DIA2♭	B♭-C-D-E♭-F-G-A	C-D-E♭-F-G-A-B♭	D-E♭-F-G-A-B♭-C	E♭-F-G-A-B♭-C-D	F-G-A-B♭-C-D-E♭	G-A-B♭-C-D-E♭-F	A-B♭-C-D-E♭-F-G
DIA1♭	F-G-A-B♭-C-D-E	G-A-B♭-C-D-E-F	A♭-C-D-E-F-G	B♭-C-D-E-F-G-A	C-D-E-F-G-A-B♭	D-E-F-G-A-B♭-C	E-F-G-A-B♭-C-D

Pentatonic (PENT). A pentatonic collection is any transposition of the five "black notes" of the piano. If it is possible ascertain a centric tone (scale-degree $\hat{1}$), a pentatonic collection can be ordered as a scale in five different ways. Pentatonic collections can be identified by the lowest note in the "major" scalar ordering: 2-2-3-2-3. So, for example, PENT$_D$ is D-E-F♯-A-B.

	Major 2-2-3-2-3	2-3-2-3-2	3-2-3-2-2	2-3-2-2-3	Minor 3-2-2-3-2
PENT$_C$	C-D-E-G-A	D-E-G-A-C	E-G-A-C-D	G-A-C-D-E	A-C-D-E-G
PENT$_{C♯}$	C♯-D♯-E♯-G♯-A♯	D♯-E♯-G♯-A♯-C♯	E♯-G♯-A♯-C♯-D♯	G♯-A♯-C♯-D♯-E♯	A♯-C♯-D♯-E♯-G♯
PENT$_D$	D-E-F♯-A-B	E-F♯-A-B-D	F♯-A-B-D-E	A-B-D-E-F♯	B-D-E-F♯-A
PENT$_{E♭}$	Eb-F-G-Bb-C	F-G-Bb-C-Eb	G-Bb-C-Eb-F	Bb-C-Eb-F-G	C-Eb-F-G-Bb
PENT$_E$	E-F♯-G♯-B-C♯	F♯-G♯-B-C♯-E	G♯-B-C♯-E-F♯	B-C♯-E-F♯-G♯	C♯-E-F♯-G♯-B
PENT$_F$	F-G-A-C-D	G-A-C-D-F	A-C-D-F-G	C-D-F-G-A	D-F-G-A-C
PENT$_{F♯}$	F♯-G♯-A♯-C♯-D♯	G♯-A♯-C♯-D♯-F♯	A♯-C♯-D♯-F♯-G♯	C♯-D♯-F♯-G♯-A♯	D♯-F♯-G♯-A♯-C♯
PENT$_G$	G-A-B-D-E	A-B-D-E-G	B-D-E-G-A	D-E-G-A-B	E-G-A-B-D
PENT$_{A♭}$	Ab-Bb-C-Eb-F	Bb-C-Eb-F-Ab	C-Eb-F-Ab-Bb	Eb-F-Ab-Bb-C	F-Ab-Bb-C-Eb
PENT$_A$	A-B-C♯-E-F♯	B-C♯-E-F♯-A	C♯-E-F♯-A-B	E-F♯-A-B-C♯	F♯-A-B-C♯-E
PENT$_{B♭}$	Bb-C-D-F-G	C-D-F-G-Bb	D-F-G-Bb-C	F-G-Bb-C-D	G-Bb-C-D-F
PENT$_B$	B-C♯-D♯-F♯-G♯	C♯-D♯-F♯-G♯-B	D♯-F♯-G♯-B-C♯	F♯-G♯-B-C♯-D♯	G♯-B-C♯-D♯-F♯

Octatonic (OCT). There are three octatonic collections that can be arranged in two intervallic orderings, both of which involve alternating 1s and 2s: 1-2-1-2-1-2-1 or 2-1-2-1-2-1-2. Octatonic collections are named by their lowest semitone: OCT$_{0,1}$ (or OCT$_{C,D♭}$); OCT$_{1,2}$ (or OCT$_{C♯,D}$); OCT$_{2,3}$ (or OCT$_{D,E♭}$).

	1-2-1-2-1-2-1-2	2-1-2-1-2-1-2-1
OCT$_{CC♯}$	C–C♯–D♯–E–F♯–G–A–Bb D♯–E–F♯–G–A–Bb–C–C♯ F♯–G–A–Bb–C–C♯–D♯–E A–Bb–C–C♯–D♯–E–F♯–G	C♯–D♯–E–F♯–G–A–Bb–C E–F♯–G–A–Bb–C–C♯–D♯ G–A–Bb–C–C♯–D♯–E–F♯ Bb–C–C♯–D♯–E–F♯–G–A
OCT$_{C♯D}$	C♯–D–E–F–G–Ab–Bb–B E–F–G–Ab–Bb–B–C♯–D G–Ab–Bb–B–C♯–D–E–F Bb–B–C♯–D–E–F–G–Ab	D–E–F–G–Ab–Bb–B–C♯ F–G–Ab–Bb–B–C♯–D–E Ab–Bb–B–C♯–D–E–F–G B–C♯–D–E–F–G–Ab–Bb
OCT$_{DD♯}$	D–Eb–F–F♯–G♯–A–B–C F–F♯–G♯–A–B–C–D–Eb G♯–A–B–C–D–Eb–F–F♯ B–C–D–Eb–F–F♯–G♯–A	Eb–F–F♯–G♯–A–B–C–D F♯–G♯–A–B–C–D–Eb–F A–B–C–D–Eb–F–F♯–G♯ C–D–Eb–F–F♯–G♯–A–B

Hexatonic (HEX). There are four hexatonic collections that can be arranged in two intervallic orderings, both of which involve alternating 1s and 3s: 1-3-1-3-1-3 or 3-1-3-1-3-1. Hexatonic collections are named by their lowest semitone.

	1–3–1–3–1–3	3–1–3–1–3–1
HEX$_{CC\#}$	C–C#–E–F–G#–A E–F–G#–A–C–C# G#–A–C–C#–E–F	C#–E–F–G#–A–C F–G#–A–C–C#–E A–C–C#–E–F–G#
HEX$_{C\#D}$	C#–D–F–F#–A–Bb F–F#–A–Bb–C#–D A–Bb–C#–D–F–F#	D–F–F#–A–Bb–C# F#–A–Bb–C#–D–F Bb–C#–D–F–F#–A
HEX$_{DD\#}$	D–Eb–F#–G–Bb–B F#–G–Bb–B–D–Eb Bb–B–D–Eb–F#–G	Eb–F#–G–Bb–B–D G–Bb–B–D–Eb–F# B–D–Eb–F#–G–Bb
HEX$_{D\#E}$	D#–E–G–Ab–B–C G–Ab–B–C–D#–E B–C–D#–E–G–Ab	E–G–Ab–B–C–D# Ab–B–C–D#–E–G C–D#–E–G–Ab–B

Whole-tone (WT). There are only two whole-tone collections, and each has only one scalar ordering: 2-2-2-2-2. The "even" whole-tone collection (WT_0) contains C (pitch-class 0); the "odd" whole-tone collection (WT_1) contains C# (pitch-class 1).

	2–2–2–2–2–2
WT$_C$	C–D–E–F#–G#–A# D–E–F#–G#–A#–C E–F#–G#–A#–C–D F#–G#–A#–C–D–E G#–A#–C–D–E–F# A#–C–D–E–F#–G#
WT$_{C\#}$	C#–D#–F–G–A–B D#–F–G–A–B–C# F–G–A–B–C#–D# G–A–B–C#–D#–F A–B–C#–D#–F–G B–C#–D#–F–G–A

Triadic transformations

Triadic transformations relate a major triad to a minor triad (and vice versa) through *common-tone preserving contextual inversion* and *voice leading parsimony*. These contextual inversions invert the triad around one or two of its notes. The new notes produced by the inversion lie only one or two semitones away from the nearest notes in the other triad.

Name	Description	Contextual Inversion	Parsimonious Voice Leading	Example
P (Parallel)	Major and minor triads share the same root.	Invert around the shared perfect fifth.	One voice moves by 1 semitone.	
L (Leading-tone)	The third of a major triad becomes the root of a minor triad (and vice versa).	Invert around the shared minor third.	One voice moves by 1 semitone.	
R (Relative)	The root of a major triad becomes the third of a minor triad (and vice versa).	Invert around the shared major third.	One voice moves by 2 semitones.	
P' (Slide)	Major and minor triads share the same third.	Invert around the note that is not part of the perfect fifth.	Two voices move by 1 semitone in the same direction.	
L'	The root of a major triad becomes the fifth of a minor triad (and vice versa).	Invert around the note that is not part of the minor third.	Two voices move by 1 semitone in the same direction.	
R'	The fifth of a major triad becomes the root of a minor triad (and vice versa).	Invert around the note that is not part of the major third.	Two voices move by 2 semitones in the same direction.	

Triadic transformations may be used in chains, which often involve an alternation of two transformations. For example, there are four LP chains, each of which involves root motion by four semitones and lies within a single hexatonic collection.

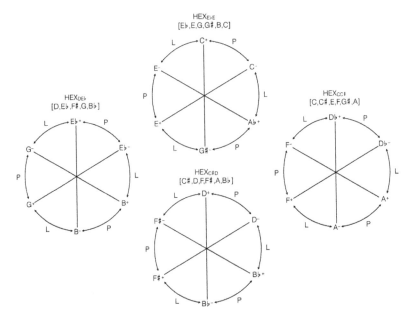

Progressions of major and minor triads can be visualized on a network called a *Tonnetz*. Major and minor triads occupy the nodes of this space and are connected by triadic transformations. Here is one possible version of such a space. LP chains (within a hexatonic collection) zigzag up and down; RP chains (within an octatonic collection) zigzag left and right; LR chains (moving through diatonic collections) occupy the NW-to-SE diagonals; P-SLIDE chains (with root motion by semitone) occupy the SW to NE diagonals.

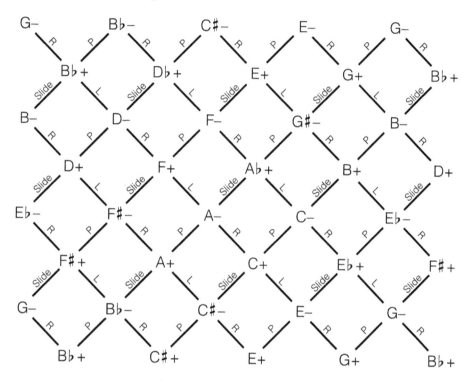

Fuzzy transposition (*T_n) and inversion (*I_n)

Chords can sometimes be productively understood as related in a manner that is very nearly transpositional or inversional. Chords related by *fuzzy transposition* or *fuzzy inversion* deviate slightly from normal, strict transposition or inversion. We will write that relationship as *T_n (x) or *I_n (x), where the asterisk denotes fuzziness and the number in parentheses indicated the number of semitones by which the relationship deviates from T_n or I_n. There will often be several possible fuzzy interpretations.

(014)   (015)
F# ——5——→ B
A ····6····→ Eb
F ——5——→ Bb

*T₅
(1)

(014)   (024)
F# ····6····→ C
A ——7——→ Bb
F ——7——→ D

*I₇
(1)

Each note moves
by some <u>interval</u>

Each note moves
by some <u>index</u> (sum)

Atonal voice leading

Whether the T and I are fuzzy or strict, the mappings they induce may be understood as transformational voices, which may or may not coincide with the registral
lines. These transformational voices will vary in perceptual strength, but provide a
systematic substrate within which, or against which, the musical lines may be heard
to move. In longer progressions involving *T and *I, the underlying arithmetic of
transposition intervals and inversion indexes will not always work out.

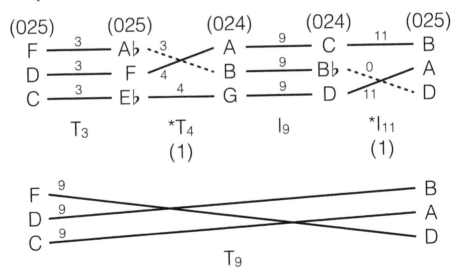

(025)   (025)   (024)   (024)   (025)
F ——3—— Ab ··3·· A ——9—— C ——11—— B
D ——3—— F ⟋4   B ——9—— Bb ··0·· A
C ——3—— Eb ——4—— G ——9—— D ⟋11·· D

T₃   *T₄   I₉   *I₁₁
             (1)   (1)

F 9 ————————————————————— B
D 9 ————————————————————— A
C 9 ————————————————————— D
        T₉

Twelve-tone series and order operations

A twelve-tone series uses each of the twelve pitch classes once, presenting them in a determinate order with a particular sequence of ordered pitch-class intervals. In addition to its original prime order (P), the series may be inverted (I), retrograded (R), and retrograde-inverted (RI), and any of these orderings may be transposed (T). For P and I forms, series are identified by their first note, using either letter names or pitch-class integers (e.g., $\boxed{P_3}$ or $\boxed{P_{E\flat}}$, $\boxed{I_7}$ or $\boxed{I_G}$). Series forms are written inside a box to distinguish them from operations: for example, $\boxed{I_3}$ is a series form, while I_3 is an operation on pitch classes, pitch-class sets, or pitch-class series.

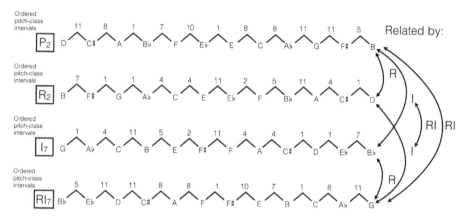

Each of these operations on the pitch classes has an effect on the intervals: transpositionally related series have the same intervals in the same order; inversionally related series (P + I, R + RI) have complementary intervals in the same order (1 becomes 11, 2 becomes 10, and so on); retrograde-related series (P + R, I and RI) have complementary intervals in reverse order; retrograde-inversionally-related series (P + RI, I + R) have the same intervals in reverse order.

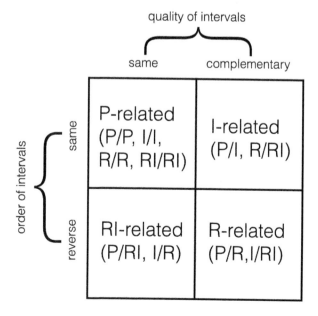

Invariance

Series forms sometimes share segmental subsets, that is, groups of adjacent notes. For example, if two trichords within a series are related at I_n, the same two trichords (in content, not order) will also be found in the I_n-related series form.

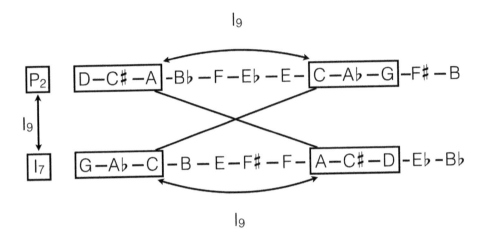

Motives and intervallic cells (serial ordering)

Two or more ordered intervals may combine into a distinctive musical shape called a *motive* or an *intervallic cell*. The intervals within a motive are enclosed within angle brackets, like <+3, -1> or <4, 11>. Usually it will be clear from context whether the intervals are pitch or pitch-class intervals. Like twelve-note series, these shorter series of pitches or pitch classes can also be reordered by inversion (I), retrograde (R), and retrograde-inversion (RI), and each of these orderings can be transposed (T). The effect on intervals is the same as for twelve-tone series.

```
  1   8              1   8
F – F♯ – D_____ Eb – E – C
            T₁₀
```

Series related by transposition.
Each pitch class transposed in order by the same interval.
Within the series: same intervals in the same order.

```
  1   8             11   4
F – F♯ – D_____ E – Eb – G
            I₉
```

Series related by inversion.
Each pitch class inverted in order by the same index.
Within the series: complementary intervals in the same order.

```
  1   8              4  11
F – F♯ – D_____ Ab – C – B
          R (at T₆)
```

Series related by retrograde.
Each pitch class inverted in reverse order by the same interval.
Within the series: complementary intervals in reverse order.

```
  1   8              8   1
F – F♯ – D_____ C♯ – A – Bb
          RI₃
```

Series related by retrograde-inversion.
Each pitch class inverted in reverse order by the same index.
Within the series: same intervals in reverse order.

Motives related by T, I, R, or RI can be presented in chains, where the final note(s) of one statement becomes the first note(s) of the next. The most prevalent is an RI-chain, where the last two notes of one motive-form become the first two notes of the one that follows, and the two are related by retrograde-inversion. Chains of this kind will eventually find their way back to their starting point (the length of the chain is determined by the intervals in the motive).

RI-chain on (014), with eight links, which starts with <8,1>.

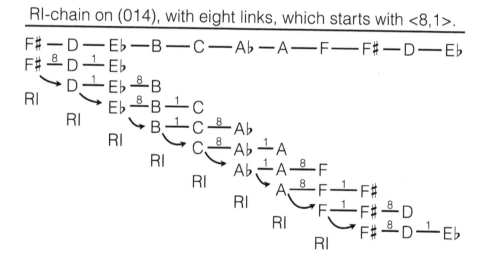

Contour

Melodic shape can be represented with a *contour-segment* (CSEG). The notes are assigned a number based on their relative registral position: 0 is assigned to the lowest note, 1 to the next lowest, and so on. The highest note will have a numerical value that is 1 less than the number of notes in the melody. The numbers are then arranged in order within angle brackets to describe the musical contour, such as <0321> for a four-note melody that begins on its lowest note, jumps to its highest note, then descends (but never gets as far back down as its starting point).

CSEG <0321>

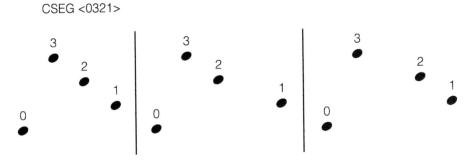

Contours related by I, R, or RI are members of a CSEG-class. There are two CSEG-classes for three-note melodies and eight CSEG-classes for four-note melodies.

CSEG-classes for three- and four-note melodies

Prime	Inversion	Retrograde	Retrograde-Inversion
<012>	<210>	Same as I	Same as P
<021>	<201>	<120>	<102>
<0123>	<3210>	Same as I	Same as P
<0132>	<3201>	<2310>	<1023>
<0213>	<3120>	Same as I	Same as P
<0231>	<3102>	<1320>	<2013>
<0312>	<3021>	<2130>	<1203>
<0321>	<3012>	<1230>	<2103>
<1032>	<2301>	Same as I	Same as P
<1302>	<2031>	Same as I	Same as P

Composing-out

There are two main ways that a motive can be expressed over both shorter and longer musical spans. First, the same pitch or pitch-class set or series may appear through two different segmentations, for example as a discrete event and in register.

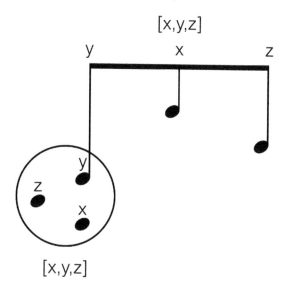

Second, the same transformations that structure the pitch classes within a set may be used to structure multiple pitch-class sets of the same type (*network isography*).

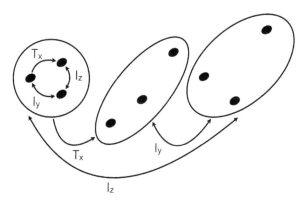

Bibliography and Suggestions for Further Reading

Post-tonal theory and analysis

Cohn, Richard. 2012. *Audacious Euphony: Chromaticism and the Triad's Second Nature*. New York: Oxford University Press.

Forte, Allen. 1973. *The Structure of Atonal Music*. New Haven, CT: Yale University Press.

Hanninen, Dora. 2012. *A Theory of Music Analysis: On Segmentation and Associative Organization*. Rochester, NY: University of Rochester Press.

Harrison, Daniel. 2016. *Pieces of Tradition: An Analysis of Contemporary Tonal Music*. New York: Oxford University Press.

Hook, Julian. 2021. *Exploring Musical Spaces*. New York: Oxford University Press.

Lewin, David. 1987. *Generalized Musical Intervals and Transformations*. New Haven, CT: Yale University Press. Reprint ed. Oxford University Press, 2011.

Lewin, David. 1993. *Musical Form and Transformation: Four Analytic Essays*. New Haven, CT: Yale University Press. Reprint ed. Oxford University Press, 2007.

Lochhead, Judith. 2016. *Reconceiving Structure in Contemporary Music: New Tools in Music Theory and Analysis*. New York: Routledge.

Morris, Robert. 1987. *Composition with Pitch Classes*. New Haven, CT: Yale University Press.

Morris, Robert. 1991. *Class Notes for Atonal Music Theory*. Lebanon, NH: Frog Peak Music.

Morris, Robert. 2001. *Class Notes for Advanced Atonal Music Theory*. Lebanon, NH: Frog Peak Music.

Parsons, Laurel and Brenda Ravenscroft, eds. 2016. *Analytical Essays on Music by Women Composers: Concert Music, 1960–2000*. New York: Oxford University Press.

Perle, George. 1991. *Serial Composition and Atonality*, 6th ed. Berkeley: University of California Press.

Rahn, John. 1980. *Basic Atonal Theory*. New York: Longman.

Roeder, John. 2014. "Transformation in Post-Tonal Music." In *Oxford Handbooks Online*. New York: Oxford University Press.

Roeder, John, Robin Attas, Mustafa Bor, Scott Alexander Cook, and Stephenie Lind. 2009. "Animating the Inside." *Music Theory Online* 15/1.

Stein, Deborah, ed. 2005. *Engaging Music: Essays in Music Analysis*. New York: Oxford University Press.

Straus, Joseph. 2016. *Introduction to Post-Tonal Theory*, 4th ed. New York: Norton.

Chapter 1. Arnold Schoenberg, *Piano Pieces*, Op. 11, No. 1

Arndt, Matthew. 2018. "Form—Function—Content." *Music Theory Spectrum* 40/2: 208–226.

Brower, Candace. 1989. "Dramatic Structure in Schoenberg's Opus 11, Number 1." *Music Research Forum* 4 (January): 25–52.

Boss, Jack. 2019. *Schoenberg's Atonal Music: Musical Idea, Basic Image, and Specters of Tonal Function*. Cambridge, UK: Cambridge University Press.

Forte, Allen. 1981. "The Magical Kaleidoscope: Schoenberg's First Atonal Masterwork, Opus 11, Number 1." *Journal of the Arnold Schoenberg Institute* 5/2: 127–168.

Haimo, Ethan. 1996. "Atonality, Analysis, and the Intentional Fallacy." *Music Theory Spectrum* 18: 167–99.

Haimo, Ethan. 2006. *Schoenberg's Transformation of Musical Language*. Cambridge, UK: Cambridge University Press.

Kurth, Richard B. 2008. "Multiple Modes of Continuity and Coherence in Schoenberg's Piano Piece, Op. 11, No. 1." In *Collected Work: Musical Currents from the Left Coast*, edited by Jack Boss and Bruce Quaglia, 282–298. Newcastle upon Tyne: Cambridge Scholars Publishing.

Lerdahl, Fred. 2001. *Tonal Pitch Space*. New York: Oxford University Press.

Lewin, David. 1998. "Some Ideas about Voice-Leading between PCSets." *Journal of Music Theory* 42/1: 15–72.

Ogdon, Will. 1981. "How Tonality Functions in Schoenberg's Opus 11, Number 1." *Journal of the Arnold Schoenberg Institute* 5/2:169–81.

Perle, George. 1990. *The Listening Composer*. Berkeley: University of California Press.

Perle, George. 1991. *Serial Composition and Atonality*, 6th ed. Berkeley: University of California Press.

Quaglia, Bruce. 2008. "Tonal Space and the 'Tonal Problem' in Schoenberg's Op. 11, No. 1." In *Collected Work: Musical Currents from the Left Coast*, edited by Jack Boss and Bruce Quaglia, 236–255. Newcastle upon Tyne: Cambridge Scholars Publishing.

Straus, Joseph. 1997. "Voice Leading in Atonal Music." In *Music Theory in Concept and Practice*, edited by James Baker, David Beach, and Jonathan Bernard, 237–274. Rochester, NY: University of Rochester Press.

Straus, Joseph. 2003. "Uniformity, Balance, and Smoothness in Atonal Voice Leading." *Music Theory Spectrum* 25/2: 305–52.

Chapter 2. Anton Webern, *Movements for String Quartet*, Op. 5, No. 2

Archibald, Bruce. 1972. "Some Thoughts on Symmetry in Early Webern: Op. 5, No. 2." *Perspectives of New Music* 10/2: 159–63.

Lewin, David. 1982–1983. "Transformational Techniques in Atonal and Other Music Theories." *Perspectives of New Music* 21: 312–29.

Roeder, John. 1995. "Voice Leading as Transformation." In *Musical Transformation and Musical Intuition: Eleven Essays in Honor of David Lewin*, edited by Raphael Atlas and Michael Cherlin, 41–58. Boston: Ovenbird Press.

Straus, Joseph. 2003. "Uniformity, Balance, and Smoothness in Atonal Voice Leading." *Music Theory Spectrum* 25/2: 305–52.

Chapter 3. Alban Berg, "Schlafend trägt man mich," from *Four Songs*, Op. 2, No. 2

Ayrey, Craig. 1982. "Berg's 'Scheideweg': Analytical Issues in Op. 2/ii." *Music Analysis* 1/2: 189–202.

Gauldin, Robert. 1999. "Reference and Association in the *Vier Lieder*, Op. 2, of Alban Berg." *Music Theory Spectrum* 21/1: 32–42.

Headlam, Dave. 1996. *The Music of Alban Berg*. New Haven, CT: Yale University Press.

Lind, Stephanie, and John Roeder. 2009. "Transformational Distance and Form in Berg's 'Schlafend trägt man mich.'" *Music Theory Online* 15.1.

Simms, Bryan R. 1992. "Alban Berg's Four Songs, Op. 2: A Tribute to Schoenberg." In *Musical Humanism and its Legacy: Essays in Honor of Claude V. Palisca*, edited by Nancy Kovaleff Baker and Barbara Russano Hanning, 487–501. Stuyvesant: Pendragon Press.

Straus, Joseph. 2011. "Contextual-Inversion Spaces." *Journal of Music Theory* 55/1: 43–88.

Tucker, Gary Richard. 2001. *Tonality and Atonality in Alban Berg's Four Songs, Op. 2*. Studies in the History and Interpretation of Music. Lewiston, NY: Edwin Mellen Press.

Chapter 4. Igor Stravinsky, *The Rite of Spring*, Introduction to Part I

Forte, Allen. 1978. *The Harmonic Organization of* The Rite of Spring. New Haven, CT: Yale University Press.

Hill, Peter. 2000. *Stravinsky: The Rite of Spring*. Cambridge University Press.

Horlacher, Gretchen. 2011. *Building Blocks: Repetition and Continuity in the Music of Stravinsky*. New York: Oxford University Press.

Katz, Adele. 1945. *Challenge to Musical Tradition: A New Concept of Tonality*. New York: Knopf. Reprint ed. Da Capo, 1972.

Russell, Jonathan. 2018. *Harmony and Voice-Leading in* The Rite of Spring. PhD dissertation. Princeton University.

Straus, Joseph. 1997. "Voice Leading in Atonal Music." In *Music Theory in Concept and Practice*, edited by James Baker, David Beach, and Jonathan Bernard, 237–274. Rochester, NY: University of Rochester Press.

Straus, Joseph. 2014. "Harmony and Voice Leading in the Music of Stravinsky." *Music Theory Spectrum*, 36/1: 1–33.

Taruskin, Richard. 1996. *Stravinsky and the Russian Traditions A Biography of the Works Through Mavra*. 2 vols. Berkeley: University of California Press.

Travis, Roy. 1959. "Toward a New Concept of Tonality." *Journal of Music Theory* 3/2: 257–84.

Van den Toorn, Pieter. 1987. *Stravinsky and the Rite of Spring: The Beginnings of a Musical Language*. Berkeley: University of California Press.

Chapter 5. Igor Stravinsky, *Three Pieces* for string quartet, No. 2

Kielian-Gilbert, Marianne. 1982–1983. "Relationships of Symmetrical Pitch-Class Sets and Stravinsky's Metaphor of Polarity." *Perspectives of New Music* 21/1–2: 209–240.

Straus, Joseph. 2018. *Broken Beauty: Musical Modernism and the Representation of Disability*. New York: Oxford University Press.

Taruskin, Richard. 1996. *Stravinsky and the Russian Traditions A Biography of the Works Through Mavra*. 2 vols. Berkeley: University of California Press.

Van den Toorn, Pieter. 1983. *The Music of Igor Stravinsky*. New Haven, CT: Yale University Press.

Chapter 6. Arnold Schoenberg, *Five Piano Pieces*, Op. 23, No. 3

Babbitt, Milton. 2003. "Since Schoenberg." In *The Collected Essays of Milton Babbitt*, edited by Peles et al., 310–334. Princeton, NJ: Princeton University Press.

Haimo, Ethan. 1990. *Schoenberg's Serial Odyssey*. Oxford, UK: Clarendon Press.

Lewin, David. 2008. "Transformational Considerations in Schoenberg's Opus 23, Number 3." In *Music Theory and Mathematics: Chords, Collections, and Transformations*, edited by Jack Douthett et al., 197–221. Rochester, NY: University of Rochester Press, 2008.

Perle, George. 1992. *Serial Composition and Atonality*, 6th ed. Berkeley: University of California Press, 1992.

Straus, Joseph. 2011. "Contextual-Inversion Spaces." *Journal of Music Theory* 55/1: 43–88.

Chapter 7. Béla Bartók, String Quartet No. 3, *Prima parte*

Antokoletz, Elliott. 1984. *The Music of Béla Bartók: A Study of Tonality and Progression in Twentieth-Century Music*. Berkeley: University of California Press.

Cohn, Richard. 1988. "Inversional Symmetry and Transpositional Combination in Bartók." *Music Theory Spectrum* 10: 19–42.

Straus, Joseph. 2008. "Motivic Chains in Bartók's Third String Quartet." *Twentieth-Century Music* 5/1: 1–20.

Straus, Joseph. 2009. "The String Quartets of Béla Bartók." In *Intimate Voices: Aspects of Construction and Character in the Twentieth-Century String Quartet*, edited by Evan Jones, 70–111. Rochester, NY: University of Rochester Press.

Chapter 8. Aaron Copland, *Piano Variations*, Theme

Simms, Bryan R. 2007. "Serialism in the Early Music of Aaron Copland." *Musical Quarterly* 90/2: 176–96.

Chapter 9. Ruth Crawford Seeger, *Diaphonic Suite No. 1*, first movement

Karpf, Juanita. 1992. "'Pleasure from the Very Smallest Things': Trichordal Transformation in Ruth Crawford's Diaphonic Suites." *Music Review* 53/1: 32–46.

Straus, Joseph. 1995. *The Music of Ruth Crawford Seeger*. Cambridge, UK: Cambridge University Press.

Tick, Judith. 1997. *Ruth Crawford Seeger: A Composer's Search for American Music*. New York: Oxford University Press.

Chapter 10. Ruth Crawford Seeger, String Quartet, first movement

Evans, Peter J. 2013. "Ruth Crawford Seeger's String Quartet 1931: Four Views of Temporal, Harmonic and Timbral Non-Coincidence." *Sonus: A Journal of Investigations into Global Musical Possibilities* 33/2: 44–55.

Greer, Taylor A. 1999. "The Dynamics of Dissonance in Seeger's Treatise and Crawford's Quartet." In *Collected Work: Understanding Charles Seeger, Pioneer in American Musicology*, 13–28. Urbana: University of Illinois Press.

Straus, Joseph. 1995. *The Music of Ruth Crawford Seeger*. Cambridge, UK: Cambridge University Press.

Tick, Judith. 1990. "Dissonant Counterpoint Revisited: The First Movement of Ruth Crawford's String Quartet 1931." In *A Celebration of Words and Music: Essays in Honor of H. Wiley Hitchcock*, edited by Richard Crawford, R. Allen Lott, and Carol Oja, 405–422. Ann Arbor: University of Michigan Press.

Tick, Judith. 1997. *Ruth Crawford Seeger: A Composer's Search for American Music*. New York: Oxford University Press.

Chapter 11. Anton Webern, "Wie bin ich froh!" from *Three Songs*, Op. 25, No. 1

Bailey, Kathryn. 1991. *The Twelve-Note Music of Anton Webern*. Cambridge, UK: Cambridge University Press.

Barry, Christopher M. 2014. "Being, Becoming, and Death in Twelve-Tone Music: 'Wie Bin Ich Froh!' As Epitaph." *Intégral* 28–29: 81–123.

Straus, Joseph. 2005. "Two Post-Tonal Analyses: Webern, 'Wie Bin Ich Froh!' from *Three Songs*, Op. 25; Schoenberg, 'Nacht,' from *Pierrot Lunaire*, Op. 21." In *Engaging Music: Essays in Music Analysis*, edited by Deborah Stein, 215–225. New York: Oxford University Press.

Chapter 12. Milton Babbitt, "The Widow's Lament in Springtime"

Mead, Andrew. 1994. *The Music of Milton Babbitt*. Princeton, NJ: Princeton University Press.
Hair, Graham and Stephen Arnold. 1969. "Some Works of Milton Babbitt." *Tempo* 90: 34–35.

Chapter 13. Luigi Dallapiccola, "Die Sonne kommt!" from *Goethe Lieder*, No. 2

Alegant, Brian. 2010. *The Twelve-Tone Music of Luigi Dallapiccola*. Rochester, NY: University of Rochester Press.
DeLio, Thomas. 1985. "A Proliferation of Canons: Luigi Dallapiccola's Goethe Lieder No. 2." *Perspectives of New Music* 23/2: 186–195.
Eckert, Michael. 1979. "Text and Form in Dallapiccola's Goethe-Lieder." *Perspectives of New Music* 17/2: 98–111.

Chapter 14. Igor Stravinsky, "Music to Hear," from *Three Shakespeare Songs*, No. 2

Babbitt, Milton. 2003. "Remarks on the Recent Stravinsky (1964)." In *The Collected Essays of Milton Babbitt*, edited by Stephen Peles et al., 147–171. Princeton, NJ: Princeton University Press.
Berry, David Carson. 2008. "The Roles of Invariance and Analogy in the Linear Design of Stravinsky's *Musick to heare*." *Gamut* 1/1 (online journal).
Groot, Rokus de. 2011. "Stravinsky's 'Musick to heare': A Study in Union and Singleness." *Dutch Journal of Music Theory* 16/1: 27–38.
Straus, Joseph. 2004. *Stravinsky's Late Music*. Cambridge, UK: Cambridge University Press.

Chapter 15. Louise Talma, "La Corona," from *Holy Sonnets*

Leonard, Kendra Preston. 2014. *Louise Talma: A Life in Composition*. London: Ashgate.

Chapter 16. Hale Smith, *Three Brevities for Solo Flute*, No. 2

Maxile, Horace. 2004. "Hale Smith's Evocation: The Interaction of Cultural Symbols and Serial Composition." *Perspectives of New Music* 42/2: 122–143.

Chapter 17. Elisabeth Lutyens, *Two Bagatelles*, Op. 48, No. 1 (1962)

Harries, Meirion and Susie Harries. 1989. *A Pilgrim Soul: The Life and Work of Elisabeth Lutyens*. London: Faber and Faber.
Parsons, Laurel. 2016. "'This Imaginary Halfe-Nothing': Temporality in Elisabeth Lutyens's *Essence of Our Happiness*." In *Analytical Essays on Music by Women Composers: Concert Music, 1960–2000* (Vol. 3), edited by Laurel Parsons and Brenda Ravenscroft, 197–220. New York: Oxford University Press.

Chapter 18. Igor Stravinsky, *Fanfare for a New Theatre*

Smyth, David. 1999. "Stravinsky's Second Crisis: Reading the Early Serial Sketches." *Perspectives of New Music* 37/2: 117–146.

Straus, Joseph. 2004. *Stravinsky's Late Music*. Cambridge, UK: Cambridge University Press.

Chapter 19. Igor Stravinsky, "Exaudi," from *Requiem Canticles*

Perry, Jeffrey. 1993. "A 'Requiem for the Requiem': On Stravinsky's Requiem Canticles." *College Music Symposium* 33–34: 237–256.

Straus, Joseph. 2012. "Three Stravinsky Analyses: *Petrushka*, Scene 1 (to Rehearsal No. 8), *The Rake's Progress*, Act III, Scene 3 ('In a Foolish Dream'), and *Requiem Canticles*, 'Exaudi.'" *Music Theory Online* 18/4 (online journal).

Straus, Joseph. 2004. *Stravinsky's Late Music*. Cambridge, UK: Cambridge University Press.

Chapter 20. Ursula Mamlok, *Panta Rhei* for piano, violin, and cello, third movement

Straus, Joseph. 2009. *Twelve-Tone Music in America*. Cambridge, UK: Cambridge University Press.

Straus, Joseph. 2016. "'Twelve-Tone in My Own Way': An Analytical Study of Ursula Mamlok's *Panta Rhei* (1981), Third Movement, with Some Reflections on Twelve-Tone Music in America." In *Analytical Essays on Music by Women Composers: Concert Music, 1960–2000* (Vol. 3), edited by Laurel Parsons and Brenda Ravenscroft, 18–31. New York: Oxford University Press.

Chapter 21. Elliott Carter, *Riconoscenza per Gofreddo Petrassi* for solo violin

Capuzzo, Guy. 2002. "Lewin's Q Operations in Carter's *Scrivo in Vento*." *Theory and Practice* 27: 85–98.

Rostron, Karen. 2016. *The Relation of Analysis to Performance of Post-Tonal Violin Music: Three Case Studies*. PhD dissertation, City University of New York.

Schiff, David. 1998. *The Music of Elliott Carter*, 2nd ed. Ithaca, NY: Cornell University Press.

Chapter 25. Kaija Saariaho, *Papillons* for solo cello, No. 3

Gainey, Christopher. 2017. "Three Approaches to Modularity in Contemporary Music." *Perspectives of New Music* 55/2: 131–166.

Roeder, John. 2016. "Superposition in Kaija Saariaho's 'The Claw of the Magnolia. . . .'" In *Analytical Essays on Music by Women Composers: Concert Music, 1960–2000* (Vol. 3), edited by Laurel Parsons and Brenda Ravenscroft, 156–175. New York: Oxford University Press.

Chapter 26. Joan Tower, *Vast Antique Cubes*

Bernard, Jonathan. 2016. "'Octatonicism,' the Octatonic Scale, and Large-Scale Structure in Joan Tower's *Silver Ladders*." In *Analytical Essays on Music by Women Composers: Concert Music, 1960–2000* (Vol. 3), edited by Laurel Parsons and Brenda Ravenscroft, 68–98. New York: Oxford University Press.

Lochhead, Judith. 1992. "Joan Tower's Wings and Breakfast Rhythms I and II: Some Thoughts on Form and Repetition." *Perspectives of New Music* 30/1: 132–56.

Chapter 27. John Adams, *On the Transmigration of Souls*

Johnson, Timothy A. 1993. "Harmonic Vocabulary in the Music of John Adams: A Hierarchical Approach." *Journal of Music Theory* 37/1: 117–156.

May, Thomas, ed. 2006. *The John Adams Reader: Essential Writings on an American Composer.* Pompton Plains, NJ: Amadeus Press.

Chapter 28. Sofia Gubaidulina, *Reflections on the Theme B–A–C–H*

Hamer, Janice. 1994. *Sofia Gubaidulina's Compositional Strategies in the String Trio (1988) and Other Works.* PhD dissertation, City University of New York.

Lochhead, Judith. 2016. *Reconceiving Structure in Contemporary Music: New Tools in Music Theory and Analysis.* New York: Routledge.

Ewell, Philip. 2014. "The Parameter Complex in the Music of Sofia Gubaidulina." *Music Theory Online* 20/3 (online journal).

Straus, Joseph. Forthcoming 2021. "Historical and Stylistic Reconciliation in Sofia Gubaidulina's *Reflections on the Theme BACH.*" In *Analytical Approaches to Twentieth-Century Russian Music: Modernism, Tonality, Serialism,* edited by Inessa Bazayev and Chris Segall. New York, Routledge.

Chapter 29. Thomas Adès, *The Tempest*, Act III, Scene 5

Chapter 30. Thomas Adès, "Days," from *Four Quarters* for string quartet

Roeder, John. 2006. "Co-operating Continuities in the Music of Thomas Adès." *Music Analysis* 25/1–2: 121–154.

Roeder, John. 2009. "A Transformational Space Structure the Counterpoint in Adès's *Auf dem Wasser zu singen.*" *Music Theory Online* 15/1 (online journal).

Stoecker, Philip. 2014. "Aligned Cycles in Thomas Adès's Piano Quintet," *Music Analysis* 33/1: 32–64.

Stoecker, Philip. 2015. "Harmony, Voice Leading, and Cyclic Structures in Thomas Adès's 'Chori.'" *Music Theory and Analysis* 2/2: 204–218.

Stoecker, Philip. 2016. "Aligned-Cycle Spaces." *Journal of Music Theory* 60/2: 181–212.

Chapter 32. Chen Yi, *Energetic Duo* for two violins

Rao, Nancy Yunhwa. 2016. "The Transformative Power of Musical Gestures: Cultural Translation in Chen Yi's Symphony No. 2." In *Analytical Essays on Music by Women Composers: Concert Music, 1960–2000* (Vol. 3), edited by Laurel Parsons and Brenda Ravenscroft, 128–152. New York: Oxford University Press.

Index